Hiking the Escalante *in the* Grand Staircase–Escalante National
Monument *and the* Glen Canyon National Recreation Area

New Edition

# Hiking the Escalante

*in the* **Grand Staircase–Escalante National Monument**
*and the* **Glen Canyon National Recreation Area**

## Rudi Lambrechtse

*Drawings by* **Linda Stitzer**

*Maps by* **Jenny Blue**

THE UNIVERSITY OF UTAH PRESS
*Salt Lake City*

The Defiance House Man colophon is a registered trademark of the University of Utah Press. It is based on a four-foot-tall Ancient Puebloan pictograph (late PIII) near Glen Canyon, Utah.

LIBRARY OF CONGRESS CATALOGING-IN-PUBLICATION DATA

Names: Lambrechtse, Rudi, author.
Title: Hiking the Escalante in the Grand Staircase-Escalante National Monument and the Glen Canyon National Recreation Area / Rudi Lambrechtse ; drawings by Linda Stitzer ; maps by Jenny Blue.
Description: Second Edition. | Salt Lake City : The University of Utah Press, 2016 | Includes bibliographical references.

Identifiers: LCCN 2015031763
ISBN 9781607814634 (Paper : alk. paper)
ISBN 9781607814641 (Ebook)

Subjects: LCSH: Hiking—Utah—Escalante River Region—Guidebooks. | Natural history—Utah—Escalante River Region. | Escalante River Region (Utah)—Guidebooks.
Classification: LCC GV199.42.U82 E835 2015 | DDC 796.5109792—dc23
LC record available at http://lccn.loc.gov/2015031763

Printed and bound by Sheridan Books, Inc., Ann Arbor, Michigan.

*For River,*
*a friend who shares in the*
*exploration of life's journey*

# Contents

# Publisher's Note

There are many opinions on the best way to write a wilderness guide. Some say there should be no guides or even maps. At the other end of the spectrum there are those who want every step and corner described. We have taken a course somewhere between these two. Realizing there are virtually no marked trails in the Escalante country (mostly canyons that wander and have many intersections, challenging anyone to write explicit descriptions), this book includes directions to the trailhead, how to follow a particular route with choices of side canyons along the way, and occasional alternate endings. Some of the hikes may be appropriate for beginners. Some only the most experienced should attempt.

All outdoor activity involves risk, particularly in the backcountry. No guide, including this one, can describe the real, changing world, and each person's reaction to it. Neither the author nor the publisher recommend that people attempt any of these routes unless they are qualified, are knowledgeable about the risks involved, and are willing to assume all responsibilities associated with those risks.

# Preface

There is a danger in writing a guidebook that the subsequent increased use will destroy those values that attracted the reader to the area in the first place. There are two reasons for believing that this will not occur here. First is the hope that the comments about minimum-impact camping will be taken to heart. As more people use the same area, the greater the need becomes to reduce or eliminate the evidence of your visit. Second, having enjoyed the scenic wonders and reveled in the wilderness experience, people will add their voices, it is hoped, to those who are working to have this area protected as designated wilderness.

There is a growing realization that we are part of, and not above, the web of interactions that bind this earth. The idea and practice of ecological consciousness is the essence of this book. When this growing awareness is expressed in social and political action, it speaks from a broader perspective than the narrowly perceived user world of the backpacker.

The Escalante canyons remain a vibrant, spacious, and intact ecosystem. Wallace Stegner recognized the unique values of this area when he called it part of "the geography of hope." Come and share it in the same vein.

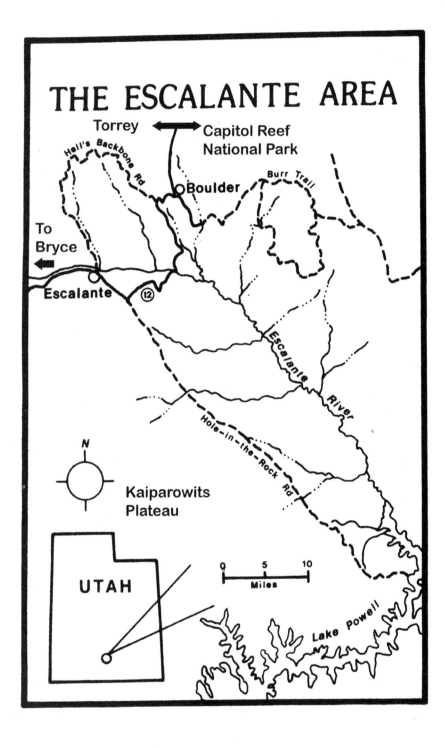

# Acknowledgments

Many people helped make this project a reality. Special thanks go to Jenny Blue, who drew the maps, Linda Stitzer, who added the drawings, and Katie Gooby, who introduced me to the original publisher.

Recognition goes to the folks at the Escalante Visitor Center for their help and support. Bill Wolverton's efforts in the canyons require a special thanks.

Thanks to my hiking companions for sharing: Betsy, Bonnie, Cal, Denise, Grant, John, John, Lewis, Linda, Mary, Mel, Mike, Mr. White, Perry Ann, River, Rufus, Sandy, Steve, Ted, and Tina.

This revised edition wouldn't have come to fruition without the guidance of John Alley and the staff at the University of Utah Press.

**PART 1**

# Background for Hiking the Escalante Area

# 1

# Walking Softly in the Wilderness

Hiking in the Escalante canyons is very different from hiking on a trail. Although there are places where use has created a noticeable path, most hikes involve a certain amount of route selection. In an attempt to minimize your impact, use existing paths wherever possible. In canyons, hike in the bottom near the stream. Cutting across benches or terraces can damage fragile desert soils and vegetation and can lead to severe erosion. In sandy areas, avoid walking on those black areas of cryptobiotic soil. This symbiotic algal and fungal covering, which looks like miniature castles, helps to stabilize the soil. The black ridges take years to form and once this bond with the soil is broken, erosion occurs rapidly.

Health and safety require the careful disposal of human waste. There are two requirements in selecting a site. First, you need to be at least three hundred feet from a water source and above the high-water mark. Second, get away from a potential camping spot. Dig a cat hole six to eight inches deep. Cover after use. Pack out your toilet paper.

No fires are allowed in the canyons, alcoves, or ruins. Use only stoves in the canyons of the monument and in Glen Canyon National Recreation Area.

Pets are not allowed in Coyote Gulch or Dry Fork. Dogs need to be on a leash elsewhere.

Practice leaving no trace. Pack it in and pack it out.

Those nighttime noises will be a lot less worrisome if you have secured your food out of the reaches of the night denizens. Most mammals, and especially the rodents, actively forage during the night. By eliminating the possibility of feeding the wild animals, you will have food to continue your journey and those wild creatures will remain exactly that. Plan meals so that you do not end up with a lot of leftovers. Food left in camp leads to the proliferation of rodents, ants, flies, and other pests.

Water is life. Since you've already paid attention to the proper disposal of your wastes, it is an easy step to not wash your dishes or use soap in the streams. You should treat all water sources. If it becomes necessary to use muddy river water, let the water settle in the container overnight and decant before treatment.

There are Native American ruins and rock art scattered throughout the canyons. These remains should give you a reason to pause and reflect on the relationships between people and their environment. In order for those who follow to have a similar experience, great care must be exercised in protecting these cultural sites. The Antiquities Act of 1916 and Archeological Resources Protection Act of 1979 make it unlawful to disturb a site or remove any artifacts, but it remains up to the will of the people to safeguard these unique areas. Never walk in, climb on, or camp in any archeological site.

The collection of rocks, petrified wood, fossils, artifacts, and plants is prohibited.

Mountain bike only on roads, not on slick-rock or cross country.

In order to have a safe and rewarding experience when hiking in this country, a person should carry the ten essentials. (This is not the place to test out new equipment. Be familiar with what you take.) The ten essentials are: a topographic map, a compass, a flashlight with spare parts, extra food and clothing, sun protection, matches, a knife, a signal mirror, a first aid kit, and an emergency shelter. There is a variety of foot gear available for walking in water. A hiking stick can come in very handy. Group size within the Monument interior is twenty-five people. More than a quarter mile from a trailhead or established parking area, the limit is twelve people.

Cattle have been removed from the Escalante River and many side drainages.

RIVER CONDITIONS: The depth of the river can vary quickly. Spring runoff can occur any time from March through May. Flash floods happen with little warning. Seek higher ground and wait for the water to recede. A walking stick can make river crossings safer. Certain side canyons require swimming. The main Escalante is boulder strewn from Scorpion Gulch to just before Stevens Canyon. Be aware of quicksand. It can be challenging but not life threatening.

HIKING SEASON: The best time to hike in the canyons is in the spring or fall. In summer there is a danger of flash floods, extreme heat, and being eaten alive by deer flies.

HIKING SAFETY: Conditions can vary radically after a storm, as well as from year to year. You should first check in at the Visitor Center west of town, where you can get the required free permits and updated weather and road condition information, and discuss your hiking ability against your projected route.

HIKING INFORMATION: Visit the Escalante Interagency Office for information, maps, books, and free camping and backpacking permits. It is located on Highway 12 on the west end of town.

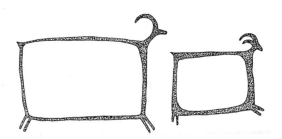

Waterfall, Deep Creek

Escalante Interagency Office
755 W. Main
P.O. Box 246
Escalante, UT 84726
435-826-5499
Email: escalante@ut.blm.gov
Open year-round, Monday–Friday, 8 am–4:30 pm
Extended hours mid-March–October, open 7 days a week, 7:30
    am–5:30 pm. (Utah goes on daylight saving time in the summer.)

The Dixie National Forest, Bureau of Land Management, and National Park Service all have their offices here. The Grand Staircase National Monument is administered by the BLM.

Dixie National Forest
P.O. Box 246
Escalante, UT 84726
435-826-5400

Bureau of Land Management
P.O. Box 225
Escalante, UT 84726
435-826-5600

National Park Service
P.O. Box 511
Escalante, UT 84726
435-826-5651
Emergency: 911
Garfield County Sheriff: 435-676-2678

Permits are also available at trailheads. There is no camping at trailheads. Information and maps can also be obtained at the Escalante Outfitters in town. Utah Canyons in the pink building across the street can also provide information and shuttles.

All maps listed at the beginning of each hike are the 7.5 topographic series.

FACILITIES: The town of Escalante has two grocery stores, three gas stations, four motels, three restaurants, a drive-in, and several bed-and-breakfasts. There is also an art gallery. Broken Bow RV Park at 495 W. Main has showers and a laundry. Cabins can be rented at the Outfitters. They also serve pizza, beer, and coffee. Utah Canyons also serves up some good coffee. There's camping and showers at the Petrified Forest State Park two miles west of town. The BLM has a campground at Calf Creek fifteen miles east of town.

The Kiva Koffeehouse and Kiva Kottage are located on Highway 12 east of town just before the road crosses the Escalante River. They serve a wonderful breakfast with a great view. They also have two rooms for rent.

The town of Boulder has two gas stations with attached grocery stores, three motels, and three places to eat. Hell's Backbone Grill is a special dining experience. The Anasazi State Park has information and is worth a visit.

# 2

# History of the Area

The earliest records were left by the Ancestral Puebloans. Remains of their brief occupation can be found throughout the area. Their history is dealt with in greater detail in chapter 5. The first recorded visit to the area by white people occurred in 1866. An uprising of Paiutes against the Mormon settlements of southern Utah and northern Arizona became known as the Black Hawk War. A group of territorial militia were called into the field and pursued the Indians. Led by Captain James Andrus, the cavalry left Kanab and traveled in a northeasterly direction. They went as far as the summit of Boulder Mountain on the eastern end of the Aquarius Plateau, crossing the upper tributaries of the Escalante River. Convinced that the Indians were safely out of southern Utah, they returned by the same route. Adjutant Franklin B. Woolley sketched a map and wrote a report of the expedition. He named the upper valley of the Escalante River "Potato Valley" because they found wild tubers growing there. His early description accurately defines the country as "cut up in all directions by these narrow deep perpendicular crevices, some of which are hundreds of feet in depth and but a rod or two in width."

John Wesley Powell led expeditions down the Colorado River in 1869 and 1871, but they did not see the mouth of the Escalante River. Members of the second expedition, led by Powell's brother-in-law, Almon H. Thompson, traversed the upper tributaries of the Escalante River in 1872 en route to retrieving a boat cached at the mouth of the Dirty Devil River. The deep gorges of the Escalante canyons also forced these explorers to detour to the north and climb the Aquarius Plateau before continuing east. Thompson realized that the drainage they were skirting was not the Dirty Devil and they had discovered a totally new river.

The name Escalante was recommended by Thompson to a group of Mormons he met at Pine Creek in 1875. Escalante was the name of

9

Mamie Creek

Old brick home in Escalante

one of the Franciscan friars who searched for a new route from Santa Fe to Monterey. In that epic journey of 1776, they explored a great deal of Utah. They passed far south of the country named after him, crossing the Colorado River in lower Glen Canyon.

For the rest of 1875, those early settlers worked on a road over Table Cliff Mountain into the upper Escalante basin. The following year work was begun on irrigation canals and a town site was laid out. Escalante's settlement differed from the pattern of other southern Utah communities where the instigating factor was a call from the church authorities. The Mormon pioneers who settled Escalante were searching for a place that had less severe weather than Panguitch. The orderly organization of the town site and the placement of the settlement near the headwaters of a river was the Mormon tradition. Lumber and dairy cattle were two early industries. At the turn of the century many fine brick homes were built, giving the town a distinctive look.

In the fall of 1879 the Hole-in-the-Rock expedition passed through the small community on its way to settle on the San Juan River in southeastern Utah. Scouts had explored longer routes through Green River or

Flagstaff, but the most direct and unexplored way was chosen. Staying west of the Escalante canyons, these pioneers blasted and constructed a precarious route for their eighty wagons and livestock through a narrow defile looking down into the Colorado River. Dance Hall Rock became the focal point for dancing and socializing while the road was being constructed. After safely getting the wagons down and across the river, the expedition struggled on through even more difficult country, arriving exhausted at the site of Bluff six months after they started.

In November of 1934, a young artist came to the Escalante canyons with a different vision. Everett Ruess had wandered extensively in the canyons of the Southwest since 1930. With a pair of burros to carry his food and art supplies, Everett went into the slick rock maze of the lower canyons. He was never seen again. A search party the next year located his burros in Davis Gulch. Several "NEMO" inscriptions were found on the canyon walls. Everett had a history of using pseudonyms. *Nemo* is the Latin word for "nobody" used by the Greek Odysseus to trick a man-eating giant. It could also refer to Captain Nemo, another person who was trying to escape from civilization, in Jules Verne's *Twenty Thousand Leagues under the Sea.*

While speculation on Ruess's disappearance continues, especially since none of his outfit was ever found, his legacy of wilderness exploration and appreciation lives on. As part of a letter written shortly before he vanished, Everett reiterates his reason for being there: "As to when I shall visit civilization, it will not be soon, I think. I have not tired of the wilderness; rather I enjoy its beauty and the vagrant life I lead, more keenly all the time. I prefer the saddle to the streetcar and the star-sprinkled sky to a roof, the obscure and difficult trail, heading into the unknown, to any paved highway, and the deep peace of the wild to the discontent bred by cities. Do you blame me then for staying here, where I feel that I belong and am one with the world around me?"

The 1930s were also a period of construction by the Civilian Conservation Corps. If the town of Escalante was difficult to get to due to the broken terrain, Boulder was at the edge of the world. The men of the CCC, based at Hungry Creek fifteen miles north of Escalante, built a road across Hell's Backbone to Boulder. The strip of road that wound precariously around the head of Death Hollow was coined "the poison road, one drop sure death." The CCC also built a recreation camp at Posey Lake and the dugway that climbs up the canyon wall by Calf Creek. This became part of the new highway to Boulder in 1940. Boulder thus ceased to be the last packhorse town.

In the 1950s, uranium exploration pushed roads into many areas. The Bureau of Land Management and Boulder stockmen worked together to construct a road from Boulder through Long Canyon into the rangeland of the Flats. This road is now part of the Burr Trail. It also provided access to the uranium mines in the Circle Cliffs.

The scenic marvels of the canyons, especially the many arches and natural bridges, slowly became known to the outside world through articles written in *National Geographic*. Most of these lower canyons were inundated when Glen Canyon Dam was completed in 1964.

On September 18, 1996, President Clinton proclaimed the establishment of the Grand Staircase–Escalante National Monument. This monument covers 1.9 million acres of southern Utah and includes a wealth of geological, biological, and archeological treasures. One of its jewels is the canyons of the Escalante.

In recent years, the diversity of hiking challenges has drawn greater numbers of backpackers into this area. It is still very similar to the description given by Clarence Dutton in 1880: "Maze of cliffs and terraces lined with stratification, of crumbling buttes, red and white domes, rock platforms gashed with profound canyons, burning plains barren even of sage, all glowing with bright color and flooded with blazing sunlight."

# AREA STRATIGRAPHY

| | | | | | |
|---|---|---|---|---|---|
| MESOZOIC | CRETACEOUS | | Kaiparowits Fm | 2700 feet | |
| | | | Wahweap Ss | 1250 | |
| | | | Straight Cliffs Fm | 1100 | |
| | | | Tropic Shale | 600 | |
| | | | Dakota Ss | 40-100 | |
| | JURASSIC | | Morrison Fm | 0-365 | |
| | | San Rafael Group | Summerville Fm | 0-145 | |
| | | | Entrada Ss | 600-750 | |
| | | | Carmel Fm | 200-400 | |
| | TRIASSIC | Glen Canyon Group | Navajo Ss | 600-1500 | |
| | | | Kayenta Fm. | 50-300 | |
| | | | Wingate Ss | 300 | |
| | | | Chinle Fm | 400 | |
| | | | Shinarump Mbr | 0-200 | |

# 3

# Geology

The Escalante Canyons are part of a large basin bounded by the Circle Cliffs and the Waterpocket Fold to the east, the Straight Cliffs to the west, and the Aquarius Plateau to the north. The Circle Cliffs and Waterpocket Fold were uplifted during the Laramide Orogeny, a period of violent geological activity that occurred fifty to eighty million years ago. The Waterpocket Fold is an extensive monocline, or buckling of the earth, that extends eighty miles from the Fremont River to Lake Powell. The Circle Cliffs are found at the western edge of the Waterpocket Fold. They have eroded into massive cliffs. The Straight Cliffs are the eastern escarpment of the Kaiparowits Plateau and extend for fifty miles from the town of Escalante to Lake Powell. The Kaiparowits and Aquarius Plateaus were also uplifted during the Laramide Orogeny. The Aquarius Plateau is a vast tableland capped by recent volcanic and glacial deposits of Cenozoic age. This plateau rises over 10,000 feet above sea level. With the uplift of the Circle Cliffs, Waterpocket Fold, and Kaiparowits and Aquarius Plateaus, the increased erosional forces cut the modern drainage pattern of the Escalante canyons.

The rocks exposed in the Escalante area were deposited during the last two eras of geological time, the Cenozoic (0–65 years before the present [YBP]) and the Mesozoic (65–230 YBP). The Mesozoic Era has been divided into three periods: the Cretaceous (65–135 YBP), the Jurassic (135–180 YBP), and the Triassic (180–230 YBP).

The rock layers exposed in the Escalante canyons were deposited during the Jurassic and Triassic Periods. The Morrison Formation, of upper Jurassic age, was deposited by streams wandering through lowlands. The sandstone and siltstone colors vary from tan to gray, purple, green, or maroon. Dinosaur fossils are frequently found in this formation. This colorful cliff-former is found west of the town of Escalante and near the base of the Straight Cliffs.

Sedimentary rocks of the San Rafael Group, of middle to late Jurassic age, consist of the Summerville Formation, Entrada Sandstone, and the Carmel Formation. The Summerville Formation varies from brown siltstones and mudstones left by the retreating Curtis Sea to yellow sandstones formed from dunes next to the tidal flats. It forms ledgy slopes to cliffs found near the base of the Straight Cliffs. The Entrada Sandstone is a reddish-tan, cross-bedded, cliff-forming sandstone. Dance Hall Rock and Chimney Rock are composed of Entrada Sandstone. The Carmel Formation consists of reddish shales, mudstones, siltstones, and gypsum. The Carmel forms a series of ledges and slopes. It is found along the Hole-in-the-Rock road at Red Breaks and the head of Twentyfive Mile Wash.

The majority of the Escalante canyons are carved into rocks of the Glen Canyon Group, of Triassic-Jurassic age. This group consists of the Navajo Sandstone, the Kayenta Formation, and the Wingate Sandstone. The Navajo Sandstone, youngest of the Glen Canyon Group, is a white to brown, cross-bedded, sandstone cliff-former that was accumulated by an eolian (windblown) environment near a marine environment. This rock erodes into fins, domes, buttes, and imposing cliffs. Arches are usually found near the base of the Navajo where it is in contact with the underlying Kayenta. The Navajo Sandstone is exposed in the Escalante Canyon walls from the town of Escalante to Horse Canyon. The Kayenta Formation forms a series of tan to maroon ledges and slopes of sandstones and siltstones. The Kayenta represents a return to fluvial or stream environments. It is found in the canyon walls of the Escalante River from Horse Canyon to Coyote Gulch. The Wingate Sandstone, oldest of the Glen Canyon Series, forms reddish-brown, cross-stratified, sandstone cliffs of eolian origin. This sandstone is subject to conchoidal fracturing such as that seen in East Moody Canyon. The Wingate is found from Choprock Bench to Coyote Gulch.

The most colorful rock formation in the area is the Triassic Chinle Formation, composed of red, brown, purple, gray, and occasionally pale green shales. This highly erodible formation contains petrified wood that

Death Hollow

was deposited along the floodplains of streams. The colors are derived from the oxides of the iron-bearing minerals. This slope-former is exposed along the base of the Circle Cliffs and at the base of the Escalante Canyon walls from Moody to Stevens Canyon.

The Shinarump Conglomerate is the basal member of the Chinle Formation and is exposed as a ledge of gray, resistant, coarse sandstone and conglomerate. A fluvial deposit, the sediment was formed by the erosion of the ancestral Rockies to the east and south. The word *shinar* means wolf in Paiute and *rump* means posterior in English. The concentration of organic debris occurred in point-bar deposits (the inner bends of meandering streams). This debris induced uranium mineralization, adding special interest wherever this layer is exposed.

Cryptobiotic soil

Eastern fence lizard

Mexican free-tailed bat

# 4

# Natural History

The Escalante canyons are part of the Colorado plateau province. While the canyons themselves are in a basin, higher land bounds the area on three sides. This broken topography creates a high degree of diversity in both the plant communities and the animal life. The top of the Aquarius Plateau, which forms the northern boundary of the Escalante basin, is over 11,000 feet above sea level. Where Lake Powell backs up into the lower canyons, the elevation is around 3,700 feet.

Besides elevation, other factors such as temperature, available moisture, soil makeup, and slope direction affect plant distribution. Mammals are not as strongly affected by such variables, but they, too, have adapted to the wide range of conditions found here. While those animals found at the higher elevations have to deal with snow and cold, those living in the lower desert have to contend with extreme summer heat.

The area contains approximately 66 species of mammals, over 150 bird species, five types of toads and frogs, nine lizards, and eleven snake species. Three of these snake species are venomous. The National Park Service has checklists for the birds and mammals of Glen Canyon National Recreation Area. While not all of the species listed are found around Escalante, they are a valuable reference.

In an attempt to place the plants in an ecological setting, a community or association will be described. For orientation, this community description will be tied to a distinct topographic feature or a specific geographical area. This will hopefully make it easier to understand your surroundings.

The northern edge of the Escalante canyons is the Aquarius Plateau. This relatively level area of lakes, meadows, and trees rises to over 11,000 feet. The southern escarpment is cut by streams that provide a continuous source of water for the Escalante River. The lakes are inhabited by cutthroat, brook, and rainbow trout. The upper part of the plateau falls in the Subalpine or Hudsonian Zone (approximately 9,500 to 11,500 feet in elevation). Also known as the spruce-fir association, Engelmann spruce and subalpine fir are the key species. Myrtle blueberry, wolf currant, and wax flower are common shrubs. Fireweed, silvery lupine, fleabane, and harebell are common meadow flowers. Mule deer, northern pocket gophers, and yellow-bellied marmots are some of the mammals. Hawks and golden eagles fly overhead, while mountain bluebirds and Cassin's finches are seen at the edge of the meadows.

Below the volcanic rim of the plateau is the fir-aspen or Canadian Zone, which covers from 8,000 to 9,500 feet in elevation. Blue spruce, quaking aspen, and Douglas fir are the dominant tree species. Common shrubs include Utah honeysuckle, elderberry, common juniper, wild raspberry, and gooseberry. Bebb and Scouler willow thickets crowd the stream banks. Beaver dams abound. Summer flowers are cranesbill, western yarrow, Columbia monkshood, sego lily, mountain gentian, and Indian paintbrush. Velvetgrass, downy brome, and the introduced wheatgrass also provide groundcover.

A variety of butterflies can be seen in the late summer. Aquatic birds such as teals, mallards, pintails, and coots utilize the marshy lakes. Broad-tailed hummingbirds, tree swallows, house wrens, yellow-bellied sapsuckers, flickers, and red-tailed hawks adorn the sky. The noisy spruce squirrel, Colorado and least chipmunks, and the golden-mantled ground squirrel are common rodents. Elk, mule deer, coyote, and beaver are among the other more visible mammals.

The next distinct topographic feature is the steep-walled canyons that drain this plateau. These include Pine Creek, Death Hollow, and Sand Creek. Portions of the Hell's Backbone road also traverse this vegetation grouping, known as the Transition Zone. The key species is the ponderosa pine tree, found roughly in the elevation range from 6,500 to 8,000 feet.

Douglas fir, Gambel oak, Rocky Mountain juniper, thin-leaf alder, and red-osier dogwood are also found here. Shrub species include point-leaf manzanita and Utah serviceberry. Shrubby cinquefoil, Fendler rose,

Coyote tracks

common aster, and wheeler thistle are common understory perennials. Grasses include redtop, wildoat, and bluegrass.

Mountain lions, mule deer, porcupines, chipmunks, and the golden-mantled ground squirrel are important mammals. Many birds are found in this forest, including the noisy, crested Stellar's jay. Mountain and western bluebirds, mountain and black-capped chickadees, Grace's warblers, western tanagers, pygmy nuthatches, broad-tailed hummingbirds, blue grouse, and a variety of owls utilize this habitat. Belted kingfishers and water ouzels are found next to the streams.

The western edge of the Escalante basin is framed by the Straight Cliffs, the eastern edge of the Kaiparowits Plateau. With the exception of Harris Wash and Collet Wash, which originate on the plateau, the rest of the streams running eastward to the Escalante River originate in the basin. The pinyon-juniper woodland type is found at the base of the Straight Cliffs. These trees are also found at the start of the Hole-in-the-Rock Road and along the drainages.

The geographical feature below the Straight Cliffs is known as desert flats, and is part of the Northern Desert Shrub Association. Most of the Hole-in-the-Rock Road traverses an area of shallow, rocky soil covered

Ord's kangaroo rat

by extensive stands of blackbrush. Mormon tea, shadscale, and broom snakeweed are other common shrubs. Around Fortymile Ridge, purple or desert sage, which is really a mint, can put on a bright blue and purple display in the spring. Where the soils are deeper and sandier, there is an increase in Indian ricegrass, dropseed, three-awn, galleta, and needle and thread grass. Narrowleaf yucca, opuntia or prickly pear, and evening primrose also dot the landscape.

Characteristic mammals of these desert flats are the coyote, black-tailed jackrabbits, Audubon cottontails, deer mice, northern grasshopper mice, little pocket mice, and Ord's kangaroo rats. In this warm climate are found such lizards as the western whiptail, side-blotched, and leopard. Loggerheaded shrikes, horned larks, and common nighthawks frequent this area. The black-throated sparrow resides in the blackbrush flats.

The Circle Cliffs are an imposing geological feature of striking colors and sharp relief on the east side of the Escalante basin. At the base of the Circle Cliffs and on the mesas and bench lands the ground is covered with pinyon and juniper trees. Local patches of Gambel oak and rabbitbrush are interspersed. Big sage occupies the floor of the Circle Cliffs basin. The canyons that drain the Circle Cliffs contain Mormon tea, yucca, serviceberry, oak, silver buffaloberry, and Palmer's penstemon.

Bighorn sheep have been reintroduced into the area, but the most common large mammal is the mule deer. Desert cottontails, black-tailed jackrabbits, Colorado chipmunks, rock squirrels, desert woodrats, white-tailed antelope squirrels, deer mice, and Ord's kangaroo rats are common. Coyotes are ubiquitous.

Typical birds are the mourning dove, scrub jay, raven, Say's phoebe, vesper sparrow, blue-gray gnatcatcher, ash-throated fly-catcher, rock wren, house finch, green-tailed towhee, pinyon jay, black-throated gray warbler, plain titmouse, and common bush tit.

The area around the town of Escalante is also part of the pinyon-juniper woodland. It is known as the pygmy forest because the trees seldom grow over thirty feet. This Upper Sonoron Zone ranges from 4,500 to 6,000 feet above sea level. In the meadows around town are western meadowlarks, magpies, Bullock's orioles, Brewer's blackbirds, and red-winged blackbirds.

The Escalante River drops two thousand feet between town and Lake Powell. A general ecological division can be made between the habitat of the canyon shelves and benches and the riparian habitat. This distinction also applies to the side canyons with flowing water.

Starting by the town, the pinyon pine and Utah junipers of the pygmy forest dominate the canyon slopes. Where the benches have accumulated sandy soil, old man sage and joint fir are found. If these areas of soil are somewhat sheltered, single-leaf ash, cliff-rose, roundleaf buffaloberry, Gambel oak, box elder, serviceberry, skunkbush sumac, Fremont barberry, desert ceanothus, and Apache plume appear. Blackbrush and big sage also intrude into this zone and can constitute important localized areas of shrub cover. The creeping vine that has distinctive white furry balls in the fall is western virgin's bower. The hedgehog cactus has a strikingly attractive red flower. Other colorful perennials are sacred datura, paintbrush, skyrocket gilia, and scarlet bugler.

Mammals frequently present but not necessarily seen include mountain lions, mule deer, gray foxes, coyotes, pinyon mice, deer mice, desert woodrats, and Ord's kangaroo rats. A variety of bat species range over the area.

When the benches become a dominant part of the canyon topography below the Gulch, big sage becomes the dominant plant. Rabbitbrush and greasewood are also found. Globe mallow adds its orange hue in the summer. Galleta, grama, and squirrel tail are common perennial grasses. These plants are one grouping of the Northern Desert Shrub Association.

Frequently seen birds include the scrub jay, ash-throated flycatcher, common bush tit, white-throated swift, canyon wren, and rock wren.

In the sand dunes around the Moody Canyons, Indian rice grass and narrow-leaf yuccas are common. The colorful shales that appear farther down-canyon support very few plants, but one of the most conspicuous is the desert trumpet, with its inflated stems.

The other major habitat in the canyons is the flowing waterway, or the riparian zone. Along the stream the Fremont cottonwood is the most frequently seen tree. Willows and salt cedar or tamarisk crowd the stream banks and the alluvial plains. Right at the stream edge, sedges, scouring rushes, saltgrass, and common horsetails abound.

Common mammals along the waterway are beaver and muskrat. Also found in the canyon are the Colorado chipmunk, cliff chipmunk, rock squirrel, brush mouse, pinyon mouse, deer mouse, and desert woodrat.

The great blue heron, snowy egret, and a variety of ducks can be found along the river. Along the canyon bottom may be seen Bullock's

oriole, house finch, yellow warbler, ash-throated flycatcher, black-headed grosbeak, broad-tailed hummingbird, and western wood pewee. The Rocky Mountain toad, red-spotted toad, Great Basin spadefoot, wandering garter snake, striped whipsnake, and gopher snake are common. Western leopard frogs are common along the lower Escalante River. The canyon treefrog is common in potholes of the lower side canyons. A special habitat found in the side canyons occurs where there is water seepage on the cliff. This can occur at any place on the cliff but usually is found near the base. It adds a spectacular contrast, especially when it is found in the overarching amphitheaters carved out of the cliff faces. This specialized community is known as the hanging garden community, and is only found in this mezic environment. The most common plant found there is maidenhair fern. Mosses and common liverworts also grow into luxuriant mats on these walls. The giant helleborine orchid, red monkey flower, cliff columbine, cardinal flower, elegant death camas, and Rydberg thistle all add color to the display.

# 5

# Prehistory

*Larry Davis, former Park Manager, Anasazi State Park*

The earliest dates for man in Utah have been obtained from excavations of cave sites in the northwestern part of the state as well as two sites in southern Utah, and place man in Utah before eight thousand years ago. The culture most evident in southern Utah is known as the Ancestral Puebloan culture and existed from about the time of Christ until A.D. 1300. During this time, the Ancestral Puebloan culture became widespread throughout the Four Corners area of the Southwest. The culture has been divided into successive time periods, the earliest of which is called Basketmaker and the last, Pueblo.

The Escalante canyons and much of the surrounding area was settled by a group or groups of ancestral Pueblo who moved to this previously unoccupied area from the San Juan River country to the southeast. Probable factors for the settlement of the area were an abundance of arable land, permanent supply of water, presence of materials for buildings, pottery, clothing, and tools, supply of firewood, and an abundance of game animals in the vicinity.

The Kayenta branch of ancestral Pueblo culture, which centered in northeastern Arizona, was the basic ingredient of this culture. Minor influences are also noted from the Mesa Verde and Chaco branches of the ancestral Pueblo culture as well as the Fremont culture to the north and east.

The archaeological evidence indicates that the area was occupied for a relatively short period of time, between A.D. 1050 and A.D. 1200.

These people were farmers, raising corn, beans, and squash. They supplemented these foodstuffs by gathering seeds, berries, and nuts. They also utilized small and large game animals for food.

Petroglyphs (Ancestral Puebloan)

The canyons were probably a year-round home for some of the ancestral Pueblo inhabitants and a seasonal home for others.

Many of the modern Pueblos living in New Mexico and Arizona are the probable descendants of the Ancestral Puebloans. The Escalante River area, like much of the entire Ancestral Puebloan area, was never again occupied by farming Indians after it was abandoned by the Ancestral Puebloans.

As you hike the many canyons of the Escalante River you will see the remnants of the Ancestral Puebloan culture. These take the form of rock art (pictographs and petroglyphs), ruins of habitation and storage structures, and simple campsites and use areas.

Both state and federal law prohibit the appropriation, excavation, injury, or destruction of any prehistoric or historic ruin or monument, or any object of antiquity. Violation and conviction under either law is subject to a fine or imprisonment, or both.

Unfortunately, a great many people are ignoring the antiquity laws and are destroying many of the archeological sites in the area through unauthorized and unscientific excavations. The "pothunting" activities are conducted by people in order to obtain artifacts to sell to collectors

Pictographs

Moqui house

and dealers. In doing so, these people vandalize and forever destroy archeological sites, making it extremely difficult to obtain scientific information from them. This makes it difficult to add to the already fascinating story of the Ancestral Puebloans.

When hiking these canyons, we ask that when you find archeological sites or objects of antiquity, you observe them and take a while to reflect back on these people and their ability to survive and adapt to this area. We would then invite you to leave these sites or objects as you found them so that others may enjoy.

A collection of Kayenta ancestral Pueblo artifacts as well as an ancestral Pueblo village may be seen at the museum and archeological site at Anasazi State Park in Boulder, Utah. The museum is open seven days a week.

**PART 2**

# Hikes

# 6

# Hikes by Degree of Difficulty and Loop Hikes

## HIKES BY DEGREE OF DIFFICULTY

## LOOP HIKES

| Name | Miles | Number of Days |
|------|-------|----------------|
| Bowns Point (HIKE 13) | 7 | 1 |
| Fence: down the Escalante River, up Twenty-five Mile (HIKE 19) | 15 | 3 to 4 |
| Fox: down the Escalante River, up Scorpion Gulch (HIKE 21, 17, 22) | 25 | 5 |
| Fortymile Ridge: up Coyote Gulch, out the Hamblin Arch route (HIKE 27, 26) | 10 | 1 to 2 |
| Fortymile Gulch: up Willow Gulch (HIKE 30, 31) | 8 | 2 to 3 |
| Deer Creek: down the Escalante River, up the Gulch (HIKE 41, 7, 42) | 35 | 6 |
| Little Death Hollow: up Wolverine Creek (HIKE 46, 45) | 13 | 1 to 2 |
| Middle Moody: up East Moody (HIKE 49, 50) | 18 | 2 to 3 |

# 7

# Highway 12

## Map, Road Log, Hikes

This is the main road into Escalante from Bryce. Extended to Boulder in 1940, it is now paved all the way to Torrey. Earlier wagon roads connecting Boulder and Escalante provide historical interest for the hikers. Directions are from the Escalante Interagency Office and Visitor Center on the west side of town.

| MILES | DESCRIPTION |
|-------|-------------|
| 0.0 | Escalante Visitor Center, heading west |
| 0.8 | Turnoff to Petrified Forest State Park (R) |
| 4.1 | Widstoe–North Creek Lakes. Turn right. |
| 4.2 | North Creek Road (R). Take this road. |
| 6.4 | North Barker Reservoir |
| 8.5 | Posey Lake Road (R). Go straight. |
| 11.3 | Road crosses North Creek. |
| 12.2 | Road crosses Twitchell Creek. The road climbs up the hill away from North Creek, with winding switchbacks. |
| 14.8 | Lower Barker Reservoir Road (R). Take this to the trailhead just past the Old Lady Group Campground in 0.5 mile. The road straight goes to the Barker Reservoir Campground. |
| | **HIKE 1: BARKER RESERVOIR** |
| 0.0 | Escalante Visitor Center, heading east |
| 1.3 | Hell's Backbone Road (L) |
| 2.0 | Unnamed road (L). Stop and read the plaque regarding the Boulder Mail Trail. Go left in 0.2 mile and follow it to the Escalante Canyons trailhead in 0.3 mile. |

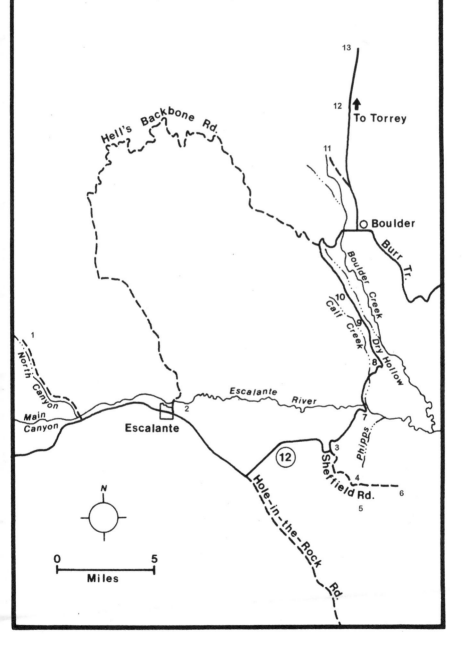

# HIGHWAY 12

13

12

To Torrey

11

Hell's Backbone Rd.

Boulder

Burr Tr.

Boulder Creek

10
Call Creek
9
Dry Hollow
8

North Canyon
1

Escalante River
2
7
Phipps

Main
Canyon
Escalante

3
12
Sheffield Rd.
4
6
5

N

Hole-in-the-Rock Rd.

0          5
Miles

**HIKE 2: ESCALANTE RIVER TO CALF CREEK** (This is also the exit for **HIKE 40: BOULDER MAIL TRAIL.**)

3.6     Airport Road (R)

6.0     Hole-in-the-Rock Road (R)

11.1    Overlook (L). Great views of the Henry Mountains to the east. The white domes immediately below you are known locally as Head of the Rocks. A portion of the old Boulder Road, known as the "Cream Cellar Route," was constructed to avoid the deep sand of Phipps pasture. It was used from 1928 to 1940 until the present highway was constructed.

11.8    Sheffield Road (R). Sam Sheffield was an early settler in the area and constructed this road to get to his homestead on the Escalante River. Also known as the Spencer Flat Road.

      0.3     **HIKE 3: PHIPPS WASH**

      2.8     **HIKE 4: BIGHORN CANYON.** Park by the juniper tree.

              **HIKE 5: CONCRETION WASH.** Park by the juniper tree.

      5.8     **HIKE 6: RED BREAKS.** Road closed at this junction.

12.9    Pullout (R). Alternate route into Phipps Wash.

15.1    Boyton Overlook (L). Good view of the Escalante River.

15.4    Kiva Koffeehouse (L)

15.8    Road crosses Escalante River. Trailhead (L). **HIKE 7: ESCALANTE RIVER: CALF CREEK TO HARRIS WASH**

17.2    Calf Creek Campground (L)

      0.4     **HIKE 8: LOWER CALF CREEK FALLS**

17.8    The road climbs sharply through the red Kayenta layer up the side of Haymaker Bench.

20.5    **HIKE 9: DRY HOLLOW–BOULDER CREEK (R)**

20.8    Great views on either side of the road as it crosses the Hogback.

| | |
|---|---|
| 23.3 | **HIKE 10: UPPER CALF CREEK FALLS (L).** Just before mile marker 81. |
| 25.7 | Hell's Backbone Road (L). Go 0.2 mile and take the first left for: HIKE 40: BOULDER MAIL TRAIL |
| 28.9 | Boulder–Burr Trail (R) |
| 34.8 | Garkane Power Plant (L) |

| | |
|---|---|
| 1.7 | Go right up the King Pasture Road. |
| 2.3 | Stay on the main road that goes right. The road gets rougher now. |
| 3.0 | Cattle guard. Road crosses the pipeline. |
| 5.6 | Unnamed road (R). This is a good place to park. Walk up this road for 0.5 mile. |

**HIKE 11: EAST BOULDER CREEK**

| | |
|---|---|
| 39.7 | **HIKE 12: DEER CREEK LAKE (L)** |
| 41.0 | Point Lookout (R). Views of the Circle Cliffs and Henry Mountains. |
| 43.5 | **HIKE 13: BOWNS POINT (L)** |
| 67.8 | Road continues to Torrey and Capitol Reef National Park. |

## HIKE 1: BARKER RESERVOIR

Difficulty: Easy
Length (one way): 3.5 miles
Time: 1 day
Maps: Barker Reservoir
Water: Old Lady Group campground and various lakes

This short loop trip takes you past five lakes and is also recommended for children. A side trip will take you through the Gap to the top of Escalante Mountain. Barker Reservoir Campground can serve as a base camp. Both the road and campground have been greatly improved from an earlier visit.

Go west from the Visitor Center on Highway 12 for 4.1 miles. Turn right and take an immediate right up North Creek Road. Barker Reservoir turnoff appears in 10.6 miles. Go right on the Lower Barker Reservoir Road for 0.5 mile to the trailhead.

Head north past the east side of Lower Barker Reservoir. Turn left on Trail #43 to Flat Lake. This small, shallow, grassy lake is tucked against the edge of Escalante Mountain. At the next trail junction, a short side trip will take you to Blue Lake, a misnomer if I ever saw one. A buck mule deer (*Odocoileus hemionus*) was having a drink when I arrived. This lake is equipped with a grill and bear-proof metal storage boxes.

The main trail skirts the southern edge of Yellow Lake. I passed the Youth Conservation Corps putting in erosion bars on this section of trail.

The next signed trail junction is Gap Trail #34. A left turn here will take you on a moderate climb up through the Gap. The trail travels along the edge of North Creek. Coming out of the Gap, follow the cairned route left up the hill to the gap trailhead sign. The track continues to FS Road 140. Here there is an expansive meadow view. The meadows are lined with spruce trees, the state tree of Colorado. The bark is gray, and the cones are longer than the similar Engelmann spruce (*Picea engelmannii*). The color of the foliage is dark green, with only the edge of the new growth exhibiting the blue color. Yellow-bellied marmots (*Marmota flaviventris*) are found among the boulders in the meadows.

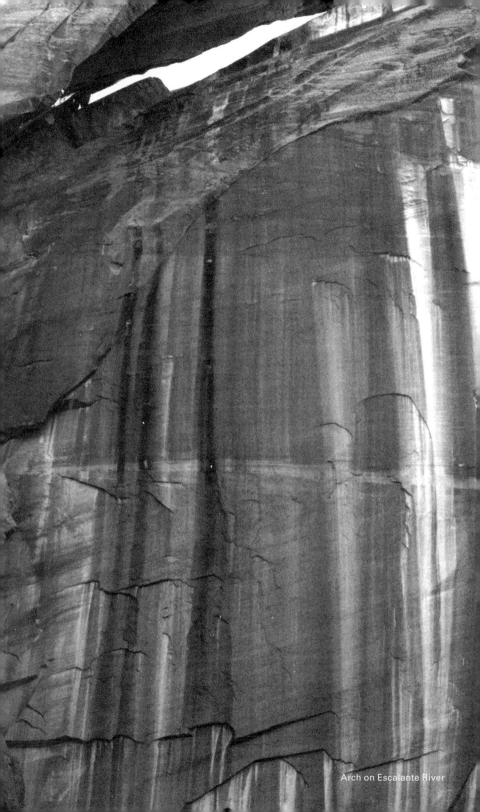

Arch on Escalante River

If you didn't do this side trip, or you are back where you first turned, follow the trail along the fence as it angles to the southwest. Blaze marks on the trees will bring you to Joe Lay Reservoir. Stay on the east side until it joins a jeep track. Follow this until it hits a "T". The route becomes a trail again heading southwest through the trees. Closing the loop, turn left at the junction, going past the east side of Lower Barker Reservoir to the trailhead.

## HIKE 2: ESCALANTE RIVER: TOWN TO CALF CREEK

Difficulty: Moderate
Length (one way): 14.9 miles
Time: 2 days
Maps: Escalante, Calf Creek
Water: Escalante River, Death Hollow, Sand Creek

This is a good introduction to hiking along the Escalante River. Usually the flow is only ankle deep. There are a variety of camp spots. The vegetation is challenging in places, but the scenery is grand. Impressive cliffs of multicolored, fissured, striated, and textured sandstone line the river. A skyline arch and natural bridge are additional interesting geological features.

Going east on Highway 12 out of Escalante, turn left by the cemetery 2 miles from the Visitor Center. Cross the cattle guard, go 0.2 mile, then turn left and go 0.3 mile more to the trailhead.

The trail skirts the cliff, avoiding the vegetation, until you hit the river.

The tilted edge of the Escalante Monocline is an imposing mass of sandstone rock. The narrow channel that the river has cut through these massive, white domes is a gateway to another world.

Almost immediately Pine Creek enters from the north, substantially adding to the volume of the river. That conical structure is the gauging station. The banks are dotted with boulders of various hues that were deposited by previous flash floods. The surrounding cliffs have cracks running in every conceivable direction. The colors of the rock vary from pure white to rust to dark brown. The black desert varnish streaks add another tone. Native Americans called this nature painting or patina. The production of these brown to black oxide stains of iron or manganese take centuries to form. Although water obviously plays a part in the creation of these streaks, the exact process is not completely understood. After an hour of walking through this sinuous portion of the canyon, you come around a bend with a low dividing ridge. The whole north wall is a sheltered overhang, a bowl scooped out of the cliff. This is one of the largest overhangs in the canyon.

Both sides of the canyon have narrow slots that drop precipitously into the main canyon. There is one on the north side that makes a sharp turn away from the river and leaves a tall bench of sandstone as foreground scenery. The backdrop is a long vertical black streak that pours over the far cliff wall.

The canyon straightens somewhat a mile before the junction with Mamie Creek. You have seen evidence of Russian olive (*Elaeagnus angustifolia*) reduction. This red-barked tree was introduced from Russia as an ornamental and windbreak. It emits a fragrant odor from its small yellow flowers. This thorny exotic is being eliminated along the river corridor by the efforts of many volunteers, initiated by Bill Wolverton, a former NPS ranger who has willingly shared his canyon knowledge.

A series of rock ledge outcroppings appears next to the bank. The rust-streaked, patterned ledges have had small pockets scooped out which have filled with small pebbles, creating miniature rock gardens. One of the drainage patterns that comes from Antone Flat enters the Escalante in a spectacular, narrow "V" high above the river.

Death Hollow enters from the north in less than a half mile. This lively stream cascades over sandstone layers. A short hike up this challenging canyon will bring you to several carved-out swimming holes. There is poison ivy along the path a half mile up. (The three-lobed, oak-like leaves are the warning sign to avoid this plant.)

By now you have passed the common trees found along a riparian habitat: willow, tamarisk, box elder, and that large, stately shade provider, the Fremont cottonwood (*Populus fremontii*). This tree is found near a water source, since it is not specifically adapted to a desert climate. It

Waterfall, Escalante River

was first described in the 1840s by John Charles Fremont, a man who certainly made his mark on western history.

What looks like a snowstorm in spring is the blowing white male catkins from the cottonwood tree. The inner bark of this tree is palatable to horses, so Fremont referred to it as sweet cottonwood. The branches are in competition with each other, so there is constant self-pruning going on in the crown.

There are shallow caves against the walls in this next section before Sand Creek. It is an easy passage from one sand bar to another. When there is a serious openness to the canyon, Sand Creek is not far away.

On the north shore, just before the stream hits the wall at the last bend before Sand Creek, a dugway has been cut going up the hill. This is a remnant of the Boynton Road, built in 1909 to serve as a shortcut between Escalante and the ranches at Salt Gulch.

A large, level, sandy area is found right at the mouth of Sand Creek. A seep is found near the mouth that provides clearer water than is usually gotten from the river. Deep pools are found a short way up this convoluted canyon.

Around the next bend of the Escalante, a huge hole is evident on the skyline. The patterns on the wall that frame this arch make this one of the most striking arches found in this canyon country. Another bend reveals Escalante Natural Bridge. A natural bridge is created by running water erosion, while an arch is formed by weathering of stressed areas of rock until a hole is formed.

The rest of the stroll to Highway 12 is along a well-worn path. A historic site that has faded with time is Phipp's grave (see HIKE 3).

Stay on the south side as you approach the bridge. There is a gate in the fence along the wall and this route respects property rights on the other bank. Cross the creek to reach the parking lot and trailhead sign.

## HIKE 3: PHIPPS WASH

Difficulty: Strenuous
Length (one way): 5.5 miles
Time: 1 day
Maps: Tenmile Flat, Calf Creek
Water: Bring your own and seasonal water in Phipps

This is a premium day hike, with a forty-foot-high arch and a natural bridge as two of the outstanding features. A colorful canyon, which usually has some water flowing near the lower end, combines challenging, slickrock hiking with an easy stroll along a willow-lined streambed. A loop trip can be made by hiking a mile up the Escalante River to Highway 12.

Follow Highway 12 east out of Escalante for 11.8 miles. Just before the road turns sharply to the left, marked with a black-and-yellow arrow highway sign, turn right onto the dirt road (this is Sheffield Road but is unmarked). There is a shallow pullout on the right in 0.3 mile.

The first challenging part of the hike is this slickrock descent to a side wash that drains into Phipps. (If this route looks too exciting for you, the

Western Screech-owl

Maverick drainage into Phipps Canyon

Phipps Arch

road log notes a place to pull off on Highway 12. This dry side fork is an easy half-mile walk and brings you to the same wash as described here.)

The road you're on is named after Sam Sheffield, an early settler who homesteaded on the Escalante River in the early 1890s. The road travels through deep sand until it reaches the rim of the Escalante River canyon, where Sheffield reportedly constructed a short log causeway to get down to a sand dune. He stayed at his farm on the river for only a few years, resettling in Boulder, where he died in 1916. The chimney is all that is left of his homestead.

The route starts due east of your car. There is an obvious "V" in the domes. Head down the slickrock of this shallow opening. When it rims out, a stair-step, slickrock descent angling to the south brings you to the sand. A dark red wall just past where you drop down is an easy landmark for the return trip.

Head down the wash in a northerly direction, passing by the side of the pour-off. The area known as "Head-of-the-Rocks" is visible as a swirling, white-domed, slickrock mass to your left. In less than a half mile you should intersect a shallow side draw. This connects to the highway as the alternate entrance.

Maverick Natural Bridge

There are several scooped-out water pockets here. On my last hike, there were two cold rattlesnakes in the first pocket. Using my hiking stick, I was able to flick them to freedom. They were only the second and third rattlesnakes I've encountered in this country in forty years.

The wash heads in an easterly direction and is easy sand hiking. When it takes an abrupt turn to the south, it is time to leave the wash. A dry waterfall stops that part of the hike. Staying on the west side, a sand dune provides easy access to the base of the waterfall. There may be a large pool of water just below this fluted jump.

A short, sandy walk brings you to the junction with the main Phipps Wash. The high walls are adorned with photogenic displays of desert varnish. When the wash heads north, a short eastern opening ends in a rincon, or hollowed area.

Heading north, water appears at ground level. Although there is still plenty of sand, the green vegetation changes the complexion of the wash.

The route up to Phipps Arch starts on the north side of the mouth of the short, eastern box canyon. Contour east and then up the ledges and slickrock. This scramble requires the use of hands in several spots. Be aware of loose rocks. The route angles northeast until it hits one of several very shallow sandstone drainages. Climb up to the upper level.

This upper level has large, pocketed sandstone domes. One of these has worn through as Phipps Arch. This majestic rock is bright orange, painted with dark streaks of desert varnish.

While I was climbing around northwest of the arch, my hat blew off into an enclosed, sandy basin. Since the walls were too steep to climb, we returned with a climbing rope. Tying off at the base of a bush, I lowered myself down what appeared to be a straight drop. Imagine my surprise when the last six feet were undercut. This small basin ended in a sheer, two-hundred-foot drop. Inspired by my lack of choice, I pulled myself and my hat back up the rope.

Sculptured water pockets and an overhanging alcove are found at the end of the box canyon just south of the arch. The main canyon has also scooped out water pockets in the red bedrock. Luxurious growth lines the bank. In the fall, the conspicuous, fluffy white balls of the western virgin's bower (*Clematis ligusticifolia*) cover the bushes. This vine clings to whatever is available. The plant was chewed by Indians and settlers as a sore throat and cold remedy.

The western drainage heads to Maverick Natural Bridge. There is a trail on the southern side that gets you out of the streambed so you can walk on top of this fin and farther up-canyon. It dead-ends in a dry waterfall in a half mile. This tributary used to be fenced at its mouth and held weaned calves.

Another mile down Phipps will bring you to the cottonwood-covered wide mouth. This wash is named after Washington Phipps, who kept a herd of horses in the area and was a partner with John Boynton, who lived a mile up the river. The partners had a falling out. Phipps threatened his former partner and was shot. His grave used to be visible upstream from Calf Creek. Boynton gave himself up, was not indicted, sold his stock, and left the area.

If you do not want to retrace your steps back up the wash, it is less than a mile up the Escalante River to Highway 12.

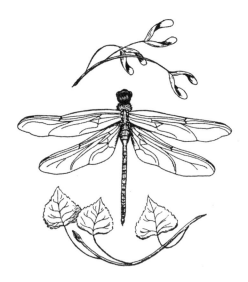

## HIKE 4: BIGHORN CANYON

Difficulty: Moderate
Length (one way): 3 miles
Time: 1 day
Map: Tenmile Flat
Water: Bring your own

This hike explores a short side drainage of Harris Wash. It has some super narrows and striated coloration similar to Zebra Slot. The narrows are best explored from the bottom.

Park on the south side of the road by the juniper. Stay this side of the post. Follow the worn path to the right of the knob into the wash. Before you reach the pour-over, climb up to the left and continue until there is a slope that you walk down to the floor of the wash. In a little over half an hour, the main canyon appears.

When the next east arm appears and the canyon slots up, there is a path above on the west (right) side. There are cairns at the corner where you drop into the wash and cross over. If you continue on the west side, the path cliffs out. Ascend the rock slope to the path that takes you high and around this section of narrows. In about twenty minutes you will drop down into the wash again until the next stupendous pour-off. Stay left to get past that plunge and narrows. Drop down the slope when it looks good (in about a half mile). Here you can walk back into the narrows for the view. You can stay in the wash for the rest of the way, walking in the sand surrounded by banded colors. The west arm just before Bighorn Canyon connects with Harris Wash and quickly becomes a narrow slot. I did this in two and a half hours to give you a time frame. Return the same way. Photography time is extra.

## HIKE 5: CONCRETION WASH

Difficulty: Moderate
Length (one way): 3.5 miles
Time: 1 day
Map: Tenmile Flat
Water: Bring your own

This has quickly become one of my favorite areas to explore, and I've given it an unofficial name. This side drainage of Harris Wash has some great sand dunes, a wonderful array of concretions, and an alternate route to Zebra Slot (HIKE 14).

Park on the south side of the road by the juniper tree. Stay east of the knob after you cross the drainage and follow the cattle track up the sand and around the southwest side of the mesa top. Drop down cross-country into the wash and follow its meanders. Skirt the first narrows on the right. Explore it from the bottom. The first sand dune appears against the west wall. The wash bends to the southwest and runs against the escarpment holding several large sand dunes.

At the next pour-off, walk the slickrock around on the left (east) side. As the wash trends southeast around a corner, there is another narrows to bypass on the east side. Pass the eastern arm and walk carefully through the concretions. There is a fence pounded into the rock at the head of Zebra Slot where you can peer down into the open bowl at its end. To explore the slot, stay high until you can drop down into Harris Wash.

## HIKE 6: RED BREAKS

Difficulty: Strenuous
Length (one way): 3.5 miles
Time: 1 day
Map: Red Breaks
Water: Bring your own

A large, raised piece of canyon country that offers many opportunities for exploration without the benefit of trails. This hike gets you to the northern end where there are domes and washes to explore. There is no specific goal for this hike, just fabulous slickrock country. This area can also be accessed from below (HIKE 16).

Park at the junction and road closure. Continue down the track to the east. In a little over a mile, a sandy track turns left. Now is the time to strike out cross-country. There may be a semblance of a track over the sand hills. Aim for the base of the escarpment, contouring east. Pass under dome 5974 along the base of this cliff face for about one and a half miles until you pass the dome marked 6015 on the topographic map. Stay below both "V" groves. Climb up the east slope of the second one to the ledge, then continue past the vegetation through the pass. Now there are choices as to what you want to explore. You can wander to the east for views of the area called the "V". You can return the same way or head northwest past the east side of dome 5975. From here you can descend to the base of the escarpment and retrace your steps to the start.

## HIKE 7: ESCALANTE RIVER: CALF CREEK TO HARRIS WASH

Difficulty: Strenuous
Length (one way): 26.4 miles
Time: 3 to 4 days
Maps: Calf Creek, King Bench, Red Breaks
Water: Escalante River, Boulder Creek, the Gulch, Harris Wash

Bowington Arch

This varied section is full of wonderful surprises. Areas with wide benches alternate with closed-in vertical walls. Side canyon exploration alone can easily double the time spent here. The ruin of a homestead settled in the 1890s adds historical flavor. Below Horse Canyon the walking becomes much easier. Exiting out Harris Wash brings you to the Hole-in-the-Rock Road and a relatively easy loop connection.

From the parking lot, cross the bridge and start down the trail on the east side of the highway. As you approach the houses (private property), veer southeast and cross the river. The fence marks the boundary of the Escalante Canyons Outstanding Natural Area. After the final crossing, you're back on the south side. The canyon already has two layers, the Kayenta ledges of reddish-purple rock found near the stream level and the domed cap rock of Navajo sandstone.

Phipps Wash (HIKE 3) is the first southern tributary. The mouth has a wide, sandy entrance, but the flowing water and the rapidly enclosing walls give this side canyon its enchantment. Cottonwood trees cover the sandy mouth, with an occasional dark red-barked tree found at streamside.

Escalante River.

Side slot                    Transverse crack

Another short side canyon comes in from the north in another mile. Known locally as Deer Canyon because of the profusion of mule deer found there, a short hike up this canyon leads to Bowington Arch. You have to bypass three small plunge pools on the way upstream. A multicolored display of boulders covers the bed of Deer Canyon between the first two pools. A short climb around the western side takes you above the third pool.

When the canyon splits, the main fork goes to the right. Bear left and the arch is visible high up in the next left spur. A scramble through the oak trees and up the sandy slope brings you almost underneath the protruding fin that contains the arch.

The main canyon remains fairly wide through here. The hardest part of the stream crossings is the slippery vegetation that grows right on the steep banks. A couple of miles above the mouth of Boulder Creek, the layered Kayenta goes underground. With only the Navajo present, the walls start to close in.

It's easy to miss the mouth of Boulder Creek, because it is well hidden by willow and tamarisk thickets. There is usually a strong flow

Author in water pocket

of water coming down this canyon. Even a short side trip up Boulder Creek (HIKE 9) reveals the scenic splendor of this very pretty canyon.

Now the willow thickets crowd the bank and make it difficult to locate and negotiate a route. The whiplash action of the willow branches is a serious obstacle to avoid. Often the route hugs the walls on the inside of

Willow thickets

the bend. Sometimes it is easier to walk down the middle of the stream. Several large sandstone blocks have separated from the wall, creating a visual discontinuity to the straight, smooth walls.

Two bends after the rockfall there is a fine campsite located on the west bank. After several more twists, a narrow crack appears on the west wall. There is no route up this, but there is a deep pool at its mouth. The cave to the north invites exploration. From here to the Gulch the canyon widens. Where the stream flows over sandstone ripples, a ledge rapid occurs in low water. The canyon appears more broken because of the perpendicular cracks running away from the stream.

When you come to the wide bend where the river doubles back on itself, there is a route out using the slot coming in from the southwest. The bend has several good campsites. This side trip is exciting, dangerous, strenuous, and geologically very interesting. With two tough scrambles, a way can be made to the slickrock expanses above the canyon.

Cross the river and head up the side stream. It ends very quickly at a pool and an impassable chute. Walk up the sand hill covered with box elder. This tree is really a maple, although the toothed leaflets are not

Side drainage narrows

Beaver cuttings

very maple-like. When yellow, these leaves readily stick to your clothing. The double-winged seeds are airborne.

Go up the rock slide in the slot farthest to the right. Carefully pick your way up until you peak out on the domed slickrock above. Head south until you can drop back down to the level of the wash. A look down the wash to where it disappears into a dark slot brings you full circle to the narrow fissure you looked at from below.

Heading up the wash, a series of plunge pools requires a detour on either side. Past these narrows, the drainage opens into a wide, sandy wash. A small natural bridge has been carved out of the bedrock. The striking red flowers of the hedgehog cactus (*Echinocereus triglochidiatus*), or claret cup, are found along this wash. These plants have adapted to the desert by storing water in their stems. This green part of the cactus also manufactures food through the photosynthetic process. Leaves have been modified to sharp spines.

Another half mile brings you to a series of cracks that take off perpendicular to the main wash. These are a series of tensional joints, caused by vertical uplift in the area. They are different from faults because there has been no vertical displacement.

The first slot to the right goes for almost a mile before a pool blocks further dry progress. The main wash dead-ends in two dry waterfalls. Continuing past the first branches, the second crack on the right is a dangerous scramble route out to the slickrock above. The silverbush or round-leaf buffaloberry (*Shepherdia rotundifolia*) that blocks the passage just before the rim needs to be carefully circumvented. Make double sure of your handholds in this chimney. The buffaloberry is an evergreen shrub with silvery coated, rounded leaves. It is the only native representative of the Oleaster family.

Another mile of walking down the widening Escalante River brings you to the mouth of the Gulch (HIKE 42). Although there is still heavy streamside vegetation, the insides of each bend are more open and passable.

The first southern bend past the Gulch has a spring where water gushes from the wall. On the north shore there is a nice beach for camping.

The river has increased in velocity in the mile or so past the Gulch. The vertical walls are offset by talus slopes at the lower part. Beaver sign is common where they have gnawed through young cottonwood trees. There are several meanders where the river almost doubles back on itself. Just before Horse Canyon, an abandoned, entrenched meander or rincon is found on the north side.

The wide mouth of Horse Canyon (HIKE 44) is also passed on the north side. Around the bend a skyline arch can be seen. From Horse to Harris the sandy benches make for an easy walk. The main struggle is finding a way through the stream-edge thickets. Once through, there is usually a well-defined path on the inside of each bend.

Isolated sandstone monoliths and sandy slopes capture the eye to the west. Going up the last sand dune and up the eight-foot wall at the rim will connect you with the old Sheffield road. Two more bends and the chimney in the large open area of Sheffield Bend is all that is left of the old homestead. After Sam Sheffield moved to Boulder, the site was lived on by a bootlegger named Bill Isabell. He remained a year or so and then also moved to Boulder.

The marshy area just west of the chimney was Sam Sheffield's water source. The mosquitoes were so thick one spring that we had to camp on the opposite shore. Following the stream up the more southerly of the alcoves visible behind the chimney leads back to a quiet amphitheater, an idyllic rest spot.

Continuing downstream, the course of the river is quite convoluted and most of your time is spent crossing the benches from one meander to the next. There may be a small amount of surface water in the first drainage coming from Big Bown Bench about a quarter mile up-canyon.

Due south across the river is a huge sand slide. The NPS has installed a new fence with a floodgate across the river in the first bend to the right past the sand slide. All fences along the river downstream have been removed. The sand slide can be used as an exit route. Several miles of westerly cross-country travel bring you to an old jeep track that ends up at the Harris trailhead.

Wall stains, Escalante River

Several more bends and Silver Falls Creek (HIKE 47) becomes visible. If you stay on the west bank across from Silver Falls, Harris Wash (HIKE 15) comes in obliquely from the northwest.

This is your exit route. If you want to continue downstream, the rest of the river route description is found in HIKE 17.

Lower Calf Creek Falls

Hedgehog cacti

Wall detail, Escalante River

Pictographs

## HIKE 8: LOWER CALF CREEK FALLS

Difficulty: Moderate
Length (one way): 2.75 miles
Time: 3 hours
Map: Calf Creek
Water: Bring your own

This sandy hike is on a self-guided nature trail along Calf Creek. Pictographs and a beautiful canyon are all part of this pleasant walk. The falls and surrounding shady pool make this an absolutely necessary trip for anyone visiting the area.

Follow the Highway 12 road log. There is a large sign indicating the turn to the BLM campground down by Calf Creek. Park by the picnic area on the right and walk down the road.

The trail starts at the sign in the campground just before the road crosses the creek. There is a box with trail pamphlets that provide interpretation for the numbered stakes along the way. This informational brochure translates the things you see so that you can have a better understanding of your surroundings.

The campground was built in 1963 with the trail to the falls completed in 1969. The time of year can affect the difficulty of the hike because most of the trail is exposed to the sun. The sandy path also adds to the difficulty of the walk. Several benches are provided as rest spots. The stream became known as Calf Creek because pioneer stockmen used this box canyon as a natural corral where calves were weaned. The shrill cries of a belted kingfisher (*Megaceryle alcyon*) can occasionally be heard as you intrude upon his fishing flights. This bird utilizes the telephone line as a perch from which to swoop along the shallow stream. The lush riparian habitat provides ample cover for a large variety of other birds.

A delightful swimming hole and 126-foot falls are found at the end of the trail. The water can be surprisingly cool and this is certainly one of the premier spots found in the canyons of the Escalante area.

## HIKE 9: DRY HOLLOW–BOULDER CREEK

Difficulty: Strenuous
Length (one way): 8 miles
Time: 1 day
Maps: Calf Creek, King Bench, Water Boulder Creek

This is an exciting hike that combines slickrock walking, struggling through thick streamside vegetation, stream wading, and some swimming. The photographic potential is excellent, ranging from large-scale views of sandstone domes to intricate streamside patterns. This trip is for experienced and adventuresome backpackers who are looking for an infrequently traveled route. The challenges of this hike are an integral part of the wilderness experience found in hiking the Escalante canyons. Except for the short section of narrows, there are numerous places to camp along the way.

Take Highway 12 east of Escalante for 19.6 miles. Where the road has just finished climbing to the top of Haymaker Bench, look for a small, sandy pullout on the right. This is the starting point, just before mile marker 79. There is a telephone pole on top of the rise right where you pull off the highway.

Lower Boulder Creek

From the pullout on the east side of Highway 12, head east down the hill. The first thirty feet or so are the most difficult as the ground is overlain with volcanic debris. Head in a southeasterly direction toward the notch where Dry Hollow joins Boulder Creek.

As you are heading down the hillside, you will cross part of the old historic Boulder Road. Access to Boulder has always been difficult, and this remnant is part of the determined pioneer transportation system. There are several colorful points of interest to the south where the road climbs a long dugway to the sandy top of Haymaker Bench. "Thompson Turnover" is a steep section of chiseled steps where Thompson's wagon did not make the sharp bend and turned over. Another area with a grade in excess of 35 percent is known as "Peter's Whip-Up." The steep grade caused James C. Peters to whip his wagon team. The horses balked and he had to bring another team the following day to retrieve his wagon.

As you are dropping down, aim for the open wash to the south. That will give you a direct line to the creek. Dry Hollow is quite brushy along the banks, so cross immediately over to the north bank and climb above the vegetation. Traverse around the convoluted, narrow plunge that Dry Hollow makes at its mouth. It is an easy descent to Boulder Creek. Take another look at the waterfall from creek level; there is a grassy spot and pool at the mouth.

Heading downstream, the scenery is dominated by white, cross-bedded rock domes. It is an easy scramble over the small saddle about one and a quarter miles down-canyon. The way becomes quite brushy as the channel narrows. Progress is slow through this stretch as you work your way along the choked banks.

In the last mile before Boulder Creek is joined by Deer Creek, the character of the canyon changes drastically. Striated sandstone ledges appear along the banks and these gentle slopes make it an easy walk.

The canyon widens perceptibly at the junction of the two creeks. There is a small overhang on the west wall that makes for a good camp spot. At two bends past the junction are the remains of an old gauging station. A dilapidated pair of hip waders and a shaky ladder complete the set. Sandstone ledges appear again but progress is slowed as you attempt to capture on film the black-and-red streaked patterns of the rock.

When the canyon heads due east, it is time for a decision. Around the corner the walls constrict and several deep plunge pools are formed by the trapped boulders. The last two of these will probably require swimming. There is an alternative route up and around these pools. Just before the south wall becomes totally straight, look for a steep slope that is possible to friction walk. There is a small vertical crack that marks the route. Directly opposite, there is a long red bench just above stream level. If that bench starts pinching out and small, sculptured alcoves appear at streamside, you've gone too far. At the top of the friction climb, a small dome will stick out to the east. To see the narrow section that is being avoided, go around the northern end of that dome and then head south. The views directly below are thrilling. Contouring in a westerly direction, there is a gradual slope back down to the creek. Cross over immediately to the east bank and there is a path for the next quarter mile.

Now the route alternates between easy benchland walking and route selection through the vegetation to effect a stream crossing. The winding course of the stream doubles back on itself several times. Then the canyon opens up with radiating side spurs to catch the eye.

The bright red berries on the lobed, currant-type leaf belongs to a shrub called skunkbush sumac (*Rhus trilobata*). The berries are edible but quite tart. With the addition of sugar they can be made into a refreshing lemonade-type drink. In the fall the leaves turn red, adding their hue to the canyon country. The name comes from the fact that Indian women made extensive use of its stems in basket weaving. This plant is also known as skunkbush, descriptive of the scent given off by the crushed leaves.

In the bends of the last mile, the canyon walls have closed in again and the stream bubbles over small rock gardens. At each sharp bend, moss is growing against the canyon wall. There is a turn to the east and Boulder Creek joins the Escalante. The mouth is brushy.

If you decide to head upstream at this point, it is 5.7 miles of hiking to reach Highway 12.

## HIKE 10: UPPER CALF CREEK FALLS

Difficulty: Moderate
Length (one way): 2 miles
Time: 1 day
Map: Calf Creek
Water: Calf Creek

A short, steep, scenic hike brings you to this waterfall, an excellent place to share a lunch and some time with a friend. Further exploration, both upstream and down, uncovers deep, inviting swimming holes.

Use the Highway 12 road log for exact mileages. Coming from Escalante, the road sits precariously on top of the Hogback. Just before the dirt road takes off to the left (milepost 80.8), the side drainage has cut back almost to the road.

From Highway 12, a short, rocky road takes you through the pinyon pine trees (*Pinus edulis*) to a wide, sandy clearing. From the trailhead marker, the hike takes off to the west next to the tallest pinyon tree at the edge of the drop-off. The state tree of New Mexico, the pinyon, burns with a fragrant smell. Good crops of the edible nuts occur every three to four years.

Sandstone detail                    Upper Calf Creek Falls

To collect these nuts, you need several lawn chairs, a large tarp, several bags, a cooler full of beer, and some straws. Lay the tarp under the tree, set up the lawn chairs, and draw straws. The short straw climbs the tree and shakes the branches so that the pine nuts fall down while the rest of the group enjoys a cold one. This procedure is repeated at different trees until enough nuts have been collected.

The view from the edge is breathtakingly similar to those snatched along the Hogback and New Home Bench. Now there is time to focus on the mass of slickrock domes, mesas, and canyon walls. The whole hillside is covered with dark, volcanic boulders. This tertiary addition occurred about 20 million years ago.

A discernible path has been created where the boulders have been moved to line the white sandstone slope. The path goes by a healthy stand of blue grama (*Bouteloua gracilis*) grass. These low clumps are easy to recognize in the fall because the seed heads look like combs. The grama grasses are an important part of most western grazing ranges.

The trail stays on the north side of the shallow draw. When trees are visible in the bowl farther down this wash, the trail contours west along the hillside. When the streaked cliff face on the west wall of Calf Creek comes into view, you should begin to hear the waterfall.

When the trail divides, the left-sloping cairned route takes you around the point and down through the vegetation to the base of the falls. The higher trail continues to the head of the falls and several deep water pockets.

The shallow overhang on the eastern side is a good place to sit and view the falls. The path continues to the grassy bank at the edge of the pool. The walls around the falls contain hanging-garden vegetation and many water streaks.

A short distance downstream, go around the pool and climb up to the cool, wet cave. Loren Eiseley said it best: "If there is magic on this earth, it lies in water." The falls and immediate surrounding area certainly contain a great deal of magic.

An excellent excursion is to follow Calf Creek for three miles downstream to the lip of Lower Calf Creek Falls. Most of the walk is in the stream, which has either a sandy or rippled sandstone bottom. Be aware of the carved-out pockets that have been eroded in the bed. These can become a sudden wet encounter if you get too engrossed in the interplay of light and shadow.

The streamside has luxurious growths of watercress (*Rorippa nasturtium-aquaticum*). This member of the Mustard family is a welcome addition to wilderness salads. The common white flower that dots the bank is Siskiyou aster (*Aster hesperius laetevirens*).

The first two side streams add substantially to the flow of water. The rock outcropping at stream level has an asymmetrical arch. In a mile, a couple of blocks of sandstone have fallen into the stream. They don't completely block the channel so they are more a visual break than an impediment to travel.

At the first western break in the wall, a nice, sheltered sandbank occurs. The cool, shady area across the stream has created a suitable microhabitat for a Douglas fir tree.

Just past the next western side draw, the streambed becomes boulder strewn and the banks get steeper. The increase in vegetation slows down progress, but a worn path on the eastern bank helps.

The final passageway before the waterfall is exciting. The stream cascades down a sandstone staircase as the walls constrict. Several deep pools have been carved out of the bedrock. A short swim is necessary to get through the last dark green pool. When that is accomplished, thirty feet more of walking brings you carefully to the edge of Lower Calf Creek Falls.

## HIKE 11: EAST BOULDER CREEK

Difficulty: Moderate
Length (one way): 7.1 mile loop
Time: 1 day
Map: Deer Creek Lake
Water: Various unnamed lakes, East Boulder Creek

This pleasant loop trip has plenty of wildflowers. The view of the Boulder Mountain escarpment at the halfway point is striking. The walk is through a mixture of meadows and wooded areas, with plenty of accessible water. Beaver (*Castor canadensis*) dams are a highlight. A side trip to Trail Point provides superlative views and is well worth the steep climb.

Continue north on Highway 12 past the Anasazi State Park for 5.2 miles. Turn left at the Garkane Power Plant sign. When the road forks, go right up the King's Pasture Road for 6.7 miles.

Although you can drive right to the trailhead sign, there are several good places to camp where the road branches and heads east. The sign to Trail Point and rock cairn just past the junction on the west side of the road is the exit point. Since the recommended hike is a loop, parking here will put you back at your car at the end of the day. Walk east up the road, passing the sign to Deer Creek Lake.

The low plant with the fern-like leaves and a small cluster of white flowers is western yarrow (*Achillea lanulosa*). Very similar to the imported eastern species (*Achillea millefolium*), the western species is native. It is named after Achilles, who reportedly discovered the healing properties of this member of the sunflower family. The Zuni applied the leaves to the skin to produce a cooling sensation.

Beaver dam, Boulder Creek

Stay on the main road heading north rather than the faint tracks turning uphill to the left. The road climbs gradually and is bounded on the left by an old log fence. To the right is a Forest Service sign indicating the start of the trail. Although it is numbered 115 on the Forest Service map, no numbers are visible on the sign. The blazed trail winds through the aspens as it climbs up the hill.

When the trail forks, follow the blazed route left and through the fence. The other trail continues to Grass Lake and dead-ends. The trail drops down to East Boulder Creek and stays on the east side of the stream. It crosses several small secondary branches and then climbs

Beaver lodge

steeply. A profusion of wildflowers grow along these brooks; especially striking is the tall, dark-blue Columbia monkshood (*Aconitum columbianum*). This flower is similar to larkspur but can be differentiated by the helmet shape of the upper sepal. All species of monkshood contain poisonous substances.

The trail wanders through the aspen and spruce trees, opening suddenly to a small lake contained by a beaver dam. I saw several families of anglers trying their luck at this pond. The trail is dotted by red Indian paintbrush. (They do look like someone dipped them in a paint bucket.) That red display consists of bracts; the flowers are white and inconspicuous.

After winding along the ridge for a short distance, the trail abruptly switches back and down the hill to a grassy lake, part of the headwaters of Boulder Creek in the summer when no more water is draining off the Aquarius Plateau. This unnamed lake is ringed on the north and west by straight volcanic cliffs and talus slopes. This escarpment is part of Boulder Mountain, at the eastern end of the Aquarius Plateau. The trail crosses the beaver dam at the southern end of the lake and then heads southwest through stands of aspen and small meadows. Ducks can be heard in the rushes, but they are well hidden. Golden columbine and harebells (*Campanula rotundifolia*) line the lake's edge. You can retrace your steps at this point but the loop trail connects you with a challenging side trail and some different scenery.

When the trail breaks through the trees and the stream reappears to the east, follow the blazes along the western edge of the meadow. The trail turns to the west at the edge of a section of private property when a house becomes visible in the distance. Within a half mile you come to the northeast corner of Divide Lake, marked by a Forest Service sign. Here a strenuous 1.7-mile side trip will take you to the top of the plateau and some striking vistas. The path going to Trail Point heads around the north side of the lake and turns abruptly to the right in about 150 feet. There is a "T" and an arrow pointing to the right, blazed into an aspen on the left side of what appears to be an old road. There is a log placed across the track marks. Look for the blazes and a fairly well-worn path.

The route goes over a short rise and then skirts a very shallow pond. There are two large volcanic rock cairns to help get you through this meadow, since the cattle paths can make the way confusing. Head north past the point of the escarpment. The trail turns west and a long, steady, steep climb will bring you to the top of the ridge.

Walk out on the boulders to the edge of the outcropping for an expansive viewpoint. West Boulder Creek is below you to the west. If your eyes follow it upstream, they will see a beautiful two-tiered waterfall where the creek cuts through the edge of the plateau. Contrasting sandstone buttes and the green area of Salt Gulch lie to the south. The East Boulder Creek drainage that you just left is directly to the east. The trail continues along the top of the plateau to Spectacle Lake, which can also be reached by Forest Service Road 162.

To complete the Boulder Creek loop, stay along the edge of Divide Lake and then head southeast down the drainage. The trail skirts the south side of the fence and is marked by a huge cairn before it crosses the road. The trail stays along the fence, then heads north and crosses Boulder Creek. On the other side it climbs the hill. Carefully cross the water pipeline that supplies the Garkane Electrical Plant. Old blaze marks on the aspen lead you east up the hill and back to the road.

Aspen on Deer Creek Lake trail

## HIKE 12: DEER CREEK LAKE

Difficulty: Easy
Length (one way): 2.7 miles
Time: 1/2 day
Maps: Deer Creek Lake, Lower Brown's Reservoir
Water: Deer Creek Lake

The trail follows an old jeep track that climbs steeply through meadows and trees. A panoramic view is available if you turn around a short distance up the trail. Deer Creek Lake is a good spot for bird-watching. Green Lake is just a little bit farther.

Continue north on the newly paved road from Boulder. There is a Forest Service sign on the left-hand side of the road indicating the turn to Deer Creek Lake. The sign is 11.1 miles north of the Anasazi State Park in Boulder. The signed road from the highway is bumpy in spots but brings you to the trailhead in a half mile. Take the right fork to the trailhead sign.

The route starts on either side of the sign and heads up the hill. The area is full of wild rose bushes. The groundcover is quite open and by turning around you have an expansive vista to the south. Immediately below, the green fields around Boulder are surrounded by white slickrock mesas. Navajo Mountain is the dominant dome far to the south.

Groundcover consists of dandelions and snakeweed (*Gutierrezia sarothrae*). This light-green member of the sunflower family has a woody base. Clusters of small, golden-yellow flowers cover the entire plant. If this plant is abundant it is considered an indicator of overgrazed land, especially by sheep. The name "snakeweed" is derived from the fact that when a sheep is bitten, a poultice is made of boiled leaves of the plant mixed with dirt. This is reported to reduce the swelling and save the sheep.

There is a junction in one and a quarter miles. The Great Western Trail goes east. We'll turn west passing two boulder-strewn depressions. The route climbs sharply into the trees, with a mix of spruce and aspen.

A golden-mantled ground squirrel (*Spermophilus lateralis*) scurried away at my approach. It is larger than the chipmunks, without the facial

Green Lake

stripes. Instead, the entire head is a coppery color. Their behavior is not as frantic as chipmunks, preferring more open country for foraging. Hibernating in the winter, the summer is spent storing food, breeding, rearing the young, and laying on fat for the next cold stretch.

Climbing over one more short rise, the path leads into a very large meadow. At the trail marker #48, turn north for a quarter mile which will bring you to the west end of Deer Creek Lake. There is a good view of the volcanic escarpment of the Aquarius Plateau.

The aspen at the edge of the meadow were alive with northern flickers. This red-winged bird has an easily distinguishable flight pattern of alternating wing beats and gliding.

Go around the west end of the lake and scramble over the boulders up to Green Lake. This narrow, deep lake is surrounded by boulders and a talus slope on the northwest side. This is the only lake I explored that resembled the cirque lakes found in the Rocky Mountains.

## HIKE 13: BOWNS POINT

Difficulty: Strenuous
Length: 7.5 mile loop
Time: 1 day
Map: Lower Bowns Reservoir
Water: Bring your own and at Long Lake

This hike starts at the fork in the road, after a half mile of high-clearance driving from Highway 12. The route is described clockwise. Follow the jeep track west through Sunflower Flat until it intersects the Great Western Trail next to the fence. Follow the track into the trees and turn up the rocky hill. Just before the track dead-ends in the trees, there is a cairn at the edge of the open area that marks the beginning of the trail. A plastic trail sign takes you northeast around the first rise. Then another brown sign leads you into the trees. Blaze marks on the aspen trees along the way keep you on course.

Over the next rise the trail turns northeast when you encounter the basalt boulder pile. Now you climb sharply up the switchbacks until you clear the rim. The map shows the pack trail continuing northwest until it intersects a jeep track at the 10,942 elevation mark. After repeated attempts, I have been unable to locate this trail. Your first choice is to head north cross-country for about a half a mile until you intersect this track. Head east and it will lead you to a stock trail that is wide and boulder strewn. The lower section was flagged over the first rise. At the base, walk along the fence until it connects with Long Lake where the jeep route takes you a mile back to the start.

The second and shorter route takes you east along the rim until you pick up a trail going east. This leads to Bowns Point. Here is an expansive view. There is a trail going down at this point past a boulder-slide area that was ablaze with white columbine in June. The trail turns left in the meadow and connects with the jeep track from Long Lake. Turn right for half a mile to the starting junction.

**8**

# Hole-in-the-Rock

## Map, Road Log, Hikes

This road provides access to the drainages on the west side of the Escalante River and terminates at the historic site of Hole-in-the-Rock. The road follows the general path taken by the San Juan Mission. This group of 250 people, answering the call of the Mormon Church to settle along the San Juan River, passed this way in 1879 and 1880. Overcoming tremendous physical barriers, they blasted a wagon route through a narrow slot at the rim of Glen Canyon. Without the loss of a single wagon they ferried the Colorado River and reached their destination after six months on the road. This is the most popular access to the Escalante Canyons.

| MILES | DESCRIPTION |
|-------|-------------|
| 0.0 | Turnoff from Highway 12 |
| 0.5 | BLM sign |
| 3.3 | Cedar Wash Road (R) |
| 8.0 | Cattle guard. **HIKE 14: HALFWAY HOLLOW–ZEBRA SLOT** |
| 10.4 | Turnoff (L) to Harris Trailhead |
| | 2.8 Cattle guard. Take the road to the left. |
| | 6.3 **HIKE 15: HARRIS WASH** |
| | **HIKE 16: RED BREAKS AGAIN** |
| | **HIKE 17: ESCALANTE RIVER: HARRIS WASH TO COYOTE GULCH** |
| 12.0 | Road (R) to Devil's Garden at 0.3 of a mile |
| | **HIKE 18: DEVIL'S GARDEN** |
| 16.4 | Egypt Turnoff (L). Road graded to this point. |
| | 8.5 Egypt sign, stay right. |
| | 10.0 **HIKE 19: FENCE CANYON** |

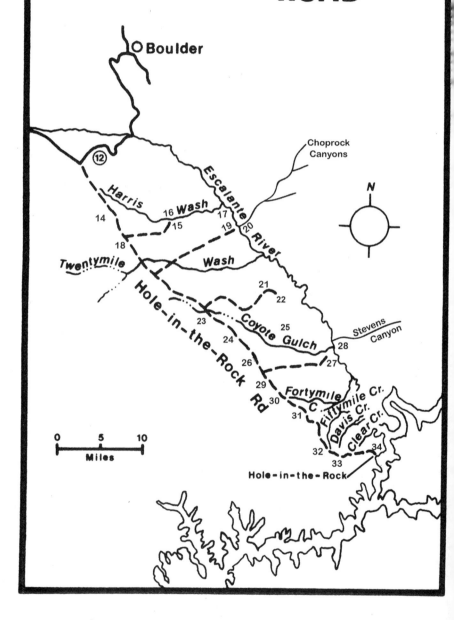

# HOLE-IN-THE-ROCK ROAD

Boulder

Choprock Canyons

N

Escalante River

Harris Wash

Twentymile Wash

Hole-in-the-Rock Rd.

Coyote Gulch

Stevens Canyon

Fortymile C.

Fiftymile Cr.

Davis Cr.

Clear Cr.

Hole-in-the-Rock

0    5    10
Miles

HIKE 20: CHOPROCK CANYONS

23.5    Early Weed Turnoff (L)

4.7    Road (L)

5.1    HIKE 21: FOX CANYON

5.6    HIKE 22: SCORPION GULCH

25.9    Dry Fork of Coyote Turnoff (L)

0.6    Take the left fork

0.7    Take the left fork

1.7    HIKE 23: DRY FORK COYOTE–PEEK-A-BOO, SPOOKY, BRIMSTONE

28.0    Cattle guard

30.6    Redwell Turnoff (L)

1.2    Take the left road.

1.3    HIKE 24: REDWELL
HIKE 25: FOOLS CANYON

31.1    Cattle guard

32.8    Chimney Rock (L). Four-wheel-drive.

33.5    Cattle guard

33.7    HIKE 26: HURRICANE WASH–COYOTE GULCH

36.0    Fortymile Ridge Road (L)

4.4    Trailhead parking left up the hill

5.0    Take left fork. Four-wheel-drive, deep sand.

7.0    HIKE 27: FORTYMILE
RIDGE–CRACK-IN-THE-WALL
HIKE 28: STEVENS CANYON

36.7    HIKE 29: DANCE HALL ROCK (L)

37.0    Cattle guard

37.4    Fortymile Spring (L)

39.4    HIKE 30: FORTYMILE GULCH. The actual drainage is Carcass Wash. Park on the right. Monument to traffic accident in 1963 that left thirteen people dead.

40.7    Sooner Rocks (R)

41.5    Turnoff to Willow Gulch (L)

1.4    HIKE 31: WILLOW GULCH

42.3    Cattle guard

| 43.3 | Fiftymile Bench Road (R). Sooner Slide |
| 45.2 | Cattle guard |
| 45.5 | **HIKE 32: FIFTYMILE CREEK.** Cave Point and caves are visible toward the west. |
| 46.2 | Glen Canyon National Recreation Area boundary sign. |
| 50.0 | Park on the spur track on the right. Look up to the top of the cliff to see the arch. **HIKE 33: DAVIS GULCH** |
| 50.3 | Cattle guard |
| 50.5 | Davis Gulch. The road shortly becomes four-wheel-drive. |
| 51.6 | Hole-in-the-Rock Arch plaque (R). You can see the arch on the skyline to the west. |
| 56.0 | This is the end of the road. **HIKE 34: HOLE-IN-THE-ROCK** |

## HIKE 14: HALFWAY HOLLOW–ZEBRA SLOT

Difficulty: Moderate
Time: 1 day
Map: Ten Mile Flat
Water: Bring your own

This short hike brings you to a narrow slot with pink-and-white stripes. There are extremely tight sections ending in a bowl and an impassable pour-off. You can also view this slot from above.

Park on the right side of the road past the cattle guard. Walk east to the cairned path across the road. Follow the wash, going through the hanging fence to Harris Wash. Go up (left) Harris Wash to the first right fork in a quarter of a mile. Walk up this sandy drainage to where it narrows. This is the entrance to the colorful Zebra slot. It will be challenging to squeeze your way through this extremely narrow space. You can also climb the slickrock to the left of the mouth and peer into it from above.

Pool at end of side canyon, Harris Wash

## HIKE 15: HARRIS WASH

Difficulty: Moderate
Length (one way): 10 miles
Time: 1 to 2 days
Maps: Red Breaks, Silver Falls Bench
Water: Harris Wash

This is a premier hike, recommended for young adults. A colorful canyon, Harris Wash provides easy access to the Escalante River. In the 1880s, this wash was part of a wagon route that led to a ferry at the mouth of Hall's Creek. There are plenty of good campsites along its winding path.

There is a sign on the Hole-in-the-Rock Road at 10.4 miles to turn left to the trailhead. From the trail register, head down the jeep track that follows the main wash. The surrounding country is wide open, with the red Carmel Formation much in evidence. Harris Wash has been closed to grazing beyond the fence since 1992. Vegetation has increased from earlier visits. In about three-quarters of a mile, the NPS boundary fence appears.

Water should be flowing in the streambed at this point. In the spring the banks are lined with smooth scouring rushes (*Equisetum laevigatum*) and field horsetails (*Equisetum arvense*). These water-loving plants provide a green tone to the streambed.

The rapid transformation of open wash to canyon occurs because the stream is down-cutting through a more resistant rock layer. In another mile a large stone fin projects from the north wall and constricts the passage to ten feet. I call this spot the portal because it feels like you are going through a gate. The immediate draw to the south invites exploration. We spotted a gopher snake just before the fluted dry waterfall. A nonvenomous snake, it is sometimes mistaken for a rattlesnake because of its diamond-shaped markings and behavioral traits of hissing and vibrating its tail. Look for the small granary on the ledge to the right. There are Moqui steps in the alcove around the corner.

As the canyon walls get higher, the winding path of the stream has cut deep overhangs. Water seeps are common along the walls of

Butte and rincon, Harris Wash

High canyon wall, Harris Wash

these alcoves. The sandy benches left by these meanders make excellent campsites. There are great displays of desert varnish on the walls.

Time goes by steadily as the walking pace is slowed to allow the senses to absorb the patterns created in this winding canyon. After three more miles a flow of water enters on the south side. This side draw is easy to miss if you are taking the high and dry path on the north side, but if you're following the stream the mouth is readily visible. The bench with oak trees is a good campsite.

The next southern side draw awaits exploration by those willing to work through the vegetation.

Another two twisting miles and a large isolated butte of sandstone on the skyline ahead indicates the junction of Harris Wash and the Escalante River.

Harris Wash was named after an early cattleman named Jimmy L. Harris. A. H. Thompson, searching for an overland route to the Dirty Devil River in 1872, called it False Creek. When the Hole-in-the-Rock route was abandoned due to lack of business, Charles Hall pioneered a wagon road to a new and easier ferry site. He operated the ferry at the mouth of Hall's Creek from 1881 to 1884. The wagon route went down Harris Wash, up Silver Falls Creek, through the Circle Cliffs, down Muley Twist Canyon, through the Water Pocket Fold, and then down Hall's Creek to its mouth at the Colorado River.

## HIKE 16: RED BREAKS AGAIN

Difficulty: Strenuous
Length (one way): 4 to 8 miles
Time: 1 to 2 days
Maps: Red Breaks
Water: Bring your own and seasonal water pockets

Off the beaten path, this area offers the challenge of narrow slot canyons, expanded vistas, and exciting cross-terrain travel. It is an area of varied and bright colors, as indicated by the name. Truly a place for those who want room to roam.

Pool and stains, Red Breaks

Follow the Hole-in-the-Rock Road log. Directions are the same as the previous hike. The route starts at the Harris Wash trailhead sign. Instead of continuing down the wash, follow the jeep road heading north. After it crosses the Harris drainage, the road will climb out of the wide, sandy wash coming down from the north. The jeep road continues out to an area called the "V," so named for the angle that Harris makes when it joins the Escalante River.

When you continue up the wash, the red-colored land is rising away from you toward the west. The walls quickly close in, and a jump blocks further wash travel in about a half mile. A short scramble up the steep, eastern stair-step wall gets you around the barrier. Bring a short piece of rope with you as it will be easier to lower your pack down before making the descent. Almost immediately there is a junction. Take the right fork up this area of smooth, layered rocks. For the next mile the wash alternates between a sand- and willow-lined bottom and sculptured rock. Finally the walls constrict so close together it's time to climb up on the right until you hit a shelf.

Carefully walk on this ledge. The views below of the slot canyon indicate an extremely tight and possibly wet walk for those intent on exploring this channel. Definitely try it without the encumbrance of a pack. In a half mile you can look across the narrow gorge to the abrupt end of a side drainage.

At the next fork a decision needs to be made concerning the route of further travel. Three choices will be outlined. There is a bit of an overhang large enough for a base camp for a small party if more than one day is going to be spent exploring the area. The first route stays on the bench land on the east side of the branch heading northeast. The walls open up in a quarter mile and there is a slickrock descent to the level wash. Now the walking becomes somewhat easier, alternating between a wide, sandy wash and slickrock. There are some interesting windblown patterns to catch and hold the eye. For the next two and a half miles, the skyline is a series of buttes, turrets, and domes—a hobbit-land display of Navajo sandstone.

At the head of the wash, where it disappears into the rocky slopes, angle north (left) and up to the dome almost directly in front of you. Skirting it on the west side, there's a shallow pass that allows access to a scenic view. Below the sloping sandstone ledges are several large, bare sand dunes. Across this open area is a domed area of joints that radiate away from the Escalante River. The laccolithic Henry Mountains rise starkly far to the north.

The second route can be used as part of a loop continuation of the first route. At the east branch junction, drop down just above its mouth. Although it is possible to slide down into the left branch at this point, it is safer and easier to immediately climb up the point between the two forks. Staying to the west, about eighty feet above the wash, there's an

Narrows, Red Breaks

easy slickrock descent in a quarter mile. You've passed the first side arm coming in from the west.

Once you're at the bottom, the amount of time since the last rain will determine how easy and dry your walk up the draw will be. After a mile of walking, there is another spur coming in from the west. A short distance up this is a small natural bridge.

The first pour-off up the main arm can be bypassed on the west side. The next constriction can be circumvented on either side. The upper portion is so narrow that you can easily step over the slot.

One more western side drainage comes in, and then a series of water pockets require slickrock walking. At the head of this wash, a walk up the tiered sandstone will bring you to the same place as the first route. You need to veer slightly to the east and around the right side of the lower knob.

The third route also goes up this western arm. After the initial descent down into the wash, immediately ascend the western side of the drainage. Contour along the western side of the rim, climbing up to the mesa top. Continuing in a northwesterly direction will put you along the rim of the arm with the natural bridge at its mouth. Follow the rim until there is a safe place to cross.

Due west of you a red knoll (X6316) breaks the skyline. This point is a mile away and about a five-hundred-foot gain in elevation. Route selection through the broken red country is up to the individual. A panoramic view presents itself as you stand on the edge of this sandstone escarpment.

Careful orienteering is necessary to find your way back. The drainages and benches look very similar. Make sure you stay far enough north to pass the head of that first side draw.

## HIKE 17: ESCALANTE RIVER: HARRIS WASH TO COYOTE GULCH

Difficulty: Strenuous
Length (one way): 43 miles
Time: 8 days
Maps: Silver Falls Bench, Egypt, Scorpion Gulch, King Meas, Stevens Canyon South
Water: Escalante River, various side drainages

This long hike can last even longer if the many tributaries are also explored. The river canyon changes from wide benches to almost barren banks to an extremely challenging, boulder-strewn section. This hike takes long enough to allow the canyon experience to envelop you.

Follow the route down Harris Wash (HIKE 15) to reach the Escalante River. Downstream from Harris Wash the river continues to meander, leaving broad, sandy areas on which to walk. Vegetative changes from the removal of cattle grazing and the reduction of Russian olive trees have altered the groundcover. The river is cutting through the softer

Kayenta Formation, which is topped by domes of Navajo sandstone. The purple of the Kayenta is offset by the light-green stems of Mormon tea (*Ephedra viridis*). These plants are first cousins to the pines and junipers. The common name is derived from brewing the tops into a drink used as a cough medicine. The drug ephedrine, used in the treatment of hay fever and colds, is obtained from some of the Asian species.

Your gentle progress along one of these benches may be interrupted by the sudden bounding gait of a blacktail jackrabbit (*Lepus californicus*). This hopper can move at speeds up to thirty-five miles per hour. The distinctive tracks show the hind feet first, followed by the unevenly spaced front paws. These hares occupy forms, or shallow depressions, rather than burrows. Their long ears are used as a thermoregulator, dissipating heat in the hot summer months.

The first western tributary appears in five and a half miles. Fence Canyon (HIKE 19) has flowing water. These side canyons are a good place to get water that is usually clearer than the river.

The Wingate sandstone frames the lower canyon walls. This colorful reddish sandstone will become imposing cliffs as the river continues down-cutting. There is a well-worn path to follow, but the brushy stream banks impede crossing from one side to the other.

Another noxious weed that scratches the legs is rattleweed milkvetch (*Astragalus praelongus*). A tall, branching plant with cream-colored flowers, the dry seedpods rattle when you pass by. Clumps of spike dropseed (*Sporobolus contractus*) dot the sandy areas. This one- to two-foot-tall grass ends in a sheathed, contracted, dense panicle of seeds. In Mesa dropseed (*Sporobolus flexuosus*) the seed head is spread in an open panicle.

In sharp contrast to the open feeling along the river, the side arms are narrow. These side branches provide a variety of experiences. Some go for a long distance, others end abruptly. Boulder strewn, dry washes, or sculpted slickrock, each has its own appeal. There is an excellent camp spot among the oaks near the mouth of the next eastern (northern) slot before Twentyfive Mile Wash. Known as Neon Canyon, access to the Golden Cathedral, it is well worth the short side hike. The mouth of Twentyfive Mile appears around the next bend as another water source.

Wall detail, Harris Wash

The first recorded traverse of the whole canyon occurred in 1939. Three Brigham Young University students were guided by Jess Barker of Escalante. They walked from Calf Creek to the Colorado River and then along the bank of the river to Hole-in-the-Rock Crossing. Here they installed a bronze plaque commemorating the trek of the San Juan Mission. The plaque was moved to the top of the notch when Lake Powell was formed.

Another six miles of meanders brings you to Moody Canyon (HIKE 48). The term "meander" is derived from the Meander River of Asia Minor, whose lower reaches have an extremely twisty course. Two more bends and a deeply cut overhang marks the mouth of East Moody Canyon (HIKE 50). There are plenty of places to camp in the sand. Water should appear in the bed of this tributary before you've gone a half mile. Several days can be spent exploring, but the conchoidal fracture displays in the Wingate walls appear a short distance up this canyon. The carved lines look like a shell, hence the name.

A half mile downstream, the river has cut through the neck of a meander, leaving a rincon. The river is quite convoluted through this section.

Scorpion Gulch (HIKE 22) is a narrow opening to the west. Good campsites are found on the sandbar at the mouth. This is another clear water source. Cattails abound in the lower end of Scorpion.

The next eastern draw is known locally as Georgie's Camp, named after Escalante stockman Geòrgie Davis. Sand dunes dominate the scenery as the canyon widens and the Wingate cliffs recede. One of the few grasses able to grow on these sandy slopes is Indian ricegrass (*Stipa hymenoides*). This grass is an extremely valuable forage plant in the semiarid West. Also used as a food source by the Indians, it was usually ground into flour and made into bread. Purple and maroon shale appears at streamside. The scenery becomes starker, and vegetation is much reduced.

For several miles this colorful display holds sway. Then around a bend a high ridge parallels the northern bank. The cliffs can be seen a half mile behind this ridge. This pile of rock reminded me of a lateral moraine left by glacial action. That certainly did not cause the deposition of this feature.

The next northern wash did not get explored very far due to the heat but looked enticing for a future trip. After the next bow-knot bend, only a low ridge and a cap rock mark the meander.

Travel down the Escalante River for fun and adventure started earlier than most people realize. In 1948, Harry Aleson and Geòrgie White Clark took the first rubber-raft trip down the Escalante. The pair had numerous adventures dealing with the changing volume of stream flow. It took them seven days to drag and float down to the swollen Colorado River, and only two more days to get to Lee's Ferry.

Stevens Arch, Escalante River

Not only for the boaters, but for hikers, the river channel becomes a test of navigational skills. Known as "The Narrows," the next five miles are extremely challenging. The way is blockaded by large boulders that have broken off the walls. A whole day can be consumed finding a way up, around, or through this boulder stretch. It is more difficult to read the river as it threads its way through these obstructions. At one crossing, I went in one step from knee-deep to chest-deep water.

The side drainages are also boulder scrambles. Just above Stevens, the canyon assumes a less broken appearance, and willow-covered banks line the stream.

Stevens Canyon (HIKE 28) is the narrow defile entering from the east. It is named for Al Stevens, who grazed cattle southwest of the Henry Mountains.

Most people head up Coyote Gulch (HIKE 26), which appears in two more bends. An alternate route into Coyote Gulch leaves from the second draw on the right past Stevens. This high-line route drops down farther up Coyote Gulch. Another alternate route out is a sand-hill climb from Coyote Gulch up the Crack-in-the-Wall route (HIKE 27). It depends on where you have arranged transport.

Travel past the mouth of Coyote varies depending on the level of the Lake Powell Reservoir.

Devil's Garden formations

## HIKE 18: DEVIL'S GARDEN

Difficulty: Easy
Length (one way): 1/2 mile
Time: 1 hour to 1/2 day
Maps: Seep Flat
Water: Bring your own

This is a fairyland area of small knobs, arches, and other eroded land-forms. The BLM recognized the scenic special features of the area and designated it as an outstanding natural area. A great place to lose yourself in flights of fantasy.

Go down the Hole-in-the-Rock Road for 12.7 miles. A BLM sign signals the short road to the right. The parking area for Devil's Garden occurs in 0.3 mile.

From the parking lot, strike out in a southerly direction. There is no trail—you can let the scenery and the topography be your guide. Mano Arch, a short distance south of the parking lot, is one of the many geological features to be viewed. These structures were formed due to a difference in the erosional rate of the different rock layers. A more resistant cap layer has protected the underlying softer rock, thus creating the many varied pinnacles.

This is an excellent area for a picnic and as much leisurely exploring as the family or group desires. A stroll around this area is unique among the outlined hikes of this guidebook because there is no set distance to go or any predetermined objective.

## HIKE 19: FENCE CANYON

Difficulty: Moderate
Length (one way): 3.5 miles
Time: 2 to 3 hours
Map: Egypt
Water: Fence Canyon

This is a short hike with outrageous views. The vista from the rim gives you a good idea of the difficulty of estimating distances and direction in this domed country. Since both arms of this canyon box out at their heads, a fence across the mouth makes this an excellent pasture. Luxurious growths along the flowing stream add to the array of colors found here.

This trailhead is located at the end of the Egypt Road, 10 miles east from the turnoff at the Hole-in-the-Rock Road. The turnoff occurs 16.4 miles down the Hole-in-the-Rock Road. There is a hiker register-box at the end of the road.

From the trailhead sign, pick up the route switching down off the rim slightly to the north (left). When the route reaches slickrock, steps have been chiseled into the rock. (This is also the stock route used by local ranchers.) After the first drop, the route seems to drop away into a series of pools. Contour south for about thirty yards on the somewhat more level sandstone until you see a narrow crack heading down. Follow the side of that crack down to the sandy wash. There may still be some cairns to guide you, but it's much better to take a route you feel safe and comfortable with.

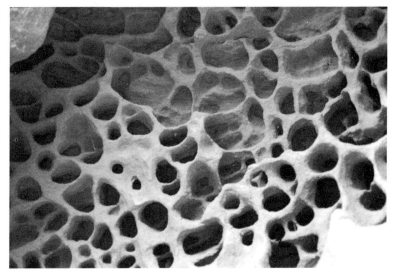

Neon Canyon wall detail

Stay in this sandy wash until it starts to notch up and drop sharply. Then cross over, finding the most level route between the sandstone domes. Travel generally northeast, but don't drift too far to the left. As you're walking over the sandy pockets, keep your bearings by staying in visual contact with the south arm of Fence Canyon on your right. There's a large alcove undercut on the south wall that is a distinctive landmark.

Continue east down to the sandy bench that is the point above where the two arms come together. The north arm should be visible, also. Angle right and down through the purple ledges. There are several paths that bring you down to the flowing water.

A well-worn path hugs the hillside, avoiding the streambed, descending before the junction with the northern arm. This branch should also have water flowing in it. If you want to explore upstream in the southern arm, stop after you've passed the first amphitheater on the north wall. If you look high and to the left, a fair-sized triangular arch should be visible just below the skyline. Passing several more alcoves on your trip upstream, the canyon comes to a beautiful, abrupt halt in another mile.

Continuing downstream past the union of the two branches, follow the path until it splits. The left branch climbs to a bench where the line

Line camp, Fence Canyon, burned in 1990

camp used to be. It also provides a view of the Escalante River. The other path takes you to the river.

To make a loop hike down the Escalante River and out Twentyfive Mile back to the trailhead, cross the river and head downstream. This three- to four-day hike is a challenging trip requiring scrambling and cross-country travel. The first stop on the east side is a look at the Baker Bench petroglyphs. You can see the evidence of an attempt to remove some of this rock art.

The first side canyon on the east side is a popular canyoneering stop. Neon Canyon and the triple natural bridges are an eye stopper. My eye also caught the Swiss cheese erosional patterns in the wall near the entrance.

In roughly 3.5 miles, there is an arch one half mile up the next east arm. After the next half mile, turn right up Twentyfive Mile Wash. Working your way up the meanders of this canyon, you'll pass the third left arm named Fox Canyon (HIKE 21).

In about a mile, a beaver pond should appear at the mouth of the right branch. Passing the pond, the wash turns south before it heads west again.

Choprock Canyon

Going just over half a mile, right after you've rounded the head of a horseshoe bend, there will be a break in the north wall. Climb up this scramble route to the top of the canyon. Aim northeast until you see the drainage in front of you that is the side arm of the beaver-pond side canyon you just passed. Cross this arm before it narrows to the west.

You can see the escarpment that is the edge of the cliff where the trailhead is. Two and a half miles of cross-country hiking will bring you to the base of that escarpment where the hike to the top will close the loop.

## HIKE 20: CHOPROCK CANYONS

Difficulty: Strenuous
Length (one way): 11 miles
Time: 3 to 4 days
Maps: Egypt, Silver Falls
Water: Escalante River, seasonal in Choprock

The Choprock Canyons have a variety of colorful delights. The mileage indicated has you starting at the Egypt trailhead and going down Fence Canyon (HIKE 19). If you are coming down the Escalante River, it will be the first open drainage on the east side after passing Harris Wash. Then the one-way distance will be about 7 miles.

When you are at the mouth of Fence Canyon, ford the river to the east side. You should be able to stay on the east side for the one and a quarter miles to the mouth of Choprock Canyon. Heading up-canyon, there are a couple of boulder piles to get by. Then there appears a large alcove with plenty of room to camp.

Another fifteen minutes brings you to the first right arm. This dead-ends shortly in a fluted pour-off.

The main canyon now offers up a pretty section of narrows. There may be water flowing here. In 1991, coming around a bend, I surprised a male bighorn sheep who quickly ran up to the rocky benchland. A couple more miles brings you to the next junction. The main fork straight ahead opens up with Wingate walls lining the passage. I didn't explore very far up this branch.

The left arm is the most interesting and challenging. It starts off easy enough but generally it's brushy and rocky. There is a good camp spot about three to four bends up. The variety continues to capture your attention: purple beds, big boulder piles, thick streamside vegetation, and benches with prickly pear cacti, junipers, and oaks. Most of the canyon is Kayenta sandstone. There is a large arch on the left wall about two hours up-canyon. It gets very rocky after that and the canyon constricts. I didn't climb the cottonwood tree trunk jammed against the lip to get up to the vertical crack that leads to a double natural bridge farther up.

## HIKE 21: FOX CANYON

Difficulty: Strenuous
Length (one way): 2 miles
Time: 1/2 day
Map: Egypt
Water: Bring your own

This short side canyon of Twentyfive Mile Wash is worth total exploration. Watch out for poison ivy. Although short, it is a cross-country route with a slickrock descent. This route down the edge of the Early Weed Bench brings you to the scenic lower portion of Twentyfive Mile Wash.

Fox Canyon is not marked on the topographic map. It is the first side canyon of Twentyfive Mile Wash inside the boundaries of Glen Canyon National Recreation Area. Proficiency in map reading and cross-country navigational skills are essential before attempting this hike.

The next short side canyon east of Fox Canyon is a box canyon, so care must be exercised to insure that you are traveling to the correct side drainage. Discuss this trip with the NPS rangers before attempting it.

The trailhead is reached by driving down the Hole-in-the-Rock Road for 23.5 miles to the Early Weed Bench sign. Turn left and be ready for the sharp turn the track makes as it crosses the wash. Continue for 5.1 miles to the trailhead register. From the parking spot, a sandstone knoll is visible on the rim directly to the east. The road continues for another half mile to parking for Scorpion Gulch (HIKE 22).

From the car, hike due north and over the edge of the rim. Descend 60 feet to a ledge of sandstone that makes walking easier. Strike off in a northwesterly direction. The route descends the slickrock escarpment, dropping over 300 feet in three quarters of a mile. Visible to the north are the steep walls of the lower portion of Fox Canyon where it joins Twentyfive Mile Wash.

As you look down toward Fox Canyon you will see a prominent butte with a brown top (5053T). Use this as a landmark as you work your way across the rolling landscape. The vertical walls of the southeast arm of Fox Canyon are also a guide.

Continue in a northwesterly direction to the head of the dry main arm of Fox Canyon. Follow the west rim of the canyon in a northeasterly direction. Another short, steep drainage will appear on your left. The rounded sandstone will lead you down to the final, steep slickrock descent to a large, sandy bench. A fifteen-foot friction walk gets you down to the sand. Locate the well-worn path that cuts back to the right down to the floor of the canyon. Watch for poison ivy as you explore both arms. A couple of bends down-canyon will bring you to the junction with Twentyfive Mile Wash.

A five-day loop hike can start here. Go down Twentyfive Mile Wash, follow the Escalante River (HIKE 17), and exit out Scorpion Gulch (HIKE 22). This wilderness loop combines a deep canyon, a long hike along the meandering river, and a scenic gulch. It exits up a sand dune, followed by strenuous cross-country hiking to return to the trailhead.

## HIKE 22: SCORPION GULCH

Difficulty: Strenuous
Length (one way): 8 miles
Time: 1 day
Maps: Egypt, Scorpion Gulch
Water: Bring your own, lower Scorpion Gulch

This exposed, five-mile cross-country route should be tried only by the physically and mentally prepared. The ability to negotiate a route across this uneven topography using the map and compass bearings is absolutely essential. Orienteering your way across open slickrock brings you to a sand slide that allows access to a very scenic side canyon of the Escalante River.

The directions are the same as the previous hike except that you drive a half mile farther to the drill pad at the end of the Early Weed Bench track.

Before starting the hike, it is valuable to lay out the topographic map and acquaint yourself with the general features to the east. To circumvent

Arch on route to Scorpion Gulch

Scorpion Gulch

the steeply eroded drainage patterns just below the rim, follow the cattle path at the end of the track around the head of Brimstone Gulch.

Head east, staying north of the promontory (5492T) visible about two miles to the east. This is the first of several such landmarks that serve as orienteering guides. The route is a mixture of sandy areas interspersed with small sandstone knolls and ridges. You'll pass just north of this outcrop, noting the small arch near the top.

You should look back to see what the topography looks like for the return trip. You'll head north of the ridge line, using knob 5524T as a guide. You'll pass south of that knob on your return.

After passing by the arch, aim for the rise marked 5025T on the map. You'll be heading just south of east. From the top of that knoll, you'll have a clear sighting of the sharp-pointed butte a mile to the southeast (Scorpion 5460). It is the tallest feature on the horizon. To the east of this butte and on the other side of Scorpion Gulch, a flat-topped mesa stands out against the skyline. (*Mesa* is the Spanish word for table, and it accurately describes this geographical feature.)

Set a line of travel that will take you a half mile north of the butte and directly toward the mesa. A mile of travel will bring you to the steep-walled canyon of Scorpion Gulch. You are north of knob 4899T. Locate the sand dune. This is your entrance down to the floor of Scorpion Gulch.

Once you are at the floor, head down-canyon. In a mile you will come to a large sand dune straddling the canyon. Upon descending this sand dune, streamside vegetation begins to appear. Large overhangs have been eroded out of the walls in this portion of Scorpion Gulch.

A half mile farther, water appears. Several large cottonwoods are growing in the bed where the water seeps out of the ground. Standing under those trees in the spring I was bombarded by the female catkins. Looking up I spotted the reason. Plumbeous vireos (*Vireo plumbeus*) were in the trees pecking at the seeds. The conspicuous white wing-bars and white eye-ring on this gray bird made identification easy.

It's a gentle walk along the stream until the northern side branch joins. Another large overhang can be seen at the base of the Navajo layer. The purple ledge layers that mark the mouth are formed by the

Cattails in Scorpion Gulch

Kayenta Formation. The resultant series of the base and sides of the stream cascades and pools add to the colorful character of this canyon.

After the dry wash comes in on the right, the canyon heads northeast again. By this time the stream has cut through the softer Kayenta layer, and Wingate sandstone forms the walls of the canyon. There are two pools in succession where large rockfalls have made travel difficult. Both of these can be bypassed on the south side by picking your way through the fallen rocks. A collared lizard was doing a pushup on one of the boulders. Its striking yellow color and two black neck bands are distinctive.

Narrows in Peek-a-boo Canyon

Below the second pool, Scorpion Gulch has a verdure tone. Cattails and other riparian vegetation choke the banks. The root stocks and young shoots of this plant were considered delicacies by Native Americans and the early settlers. When you can see the free-standing pinnacles, you're at the river and the end of the hike. There are several good camp spots at the mouth.

## HIKE 23: DRY FORK COYOTE: PEEK-A-BOO, SPOOKY, BRIMSTONE

Difficulty: Strenuous
Length (one way): 6 miles
Time: 1 day
Maps: Big Hollow Wash
Water: Bring your own

This day hike explores three narrow slots that drain the north side of Dry Fork Coyote Gulch. Peek-a-boo, Spooky, and Brimstone are challenging, claustrophobic, exciting, and fun. Caution must be exercised when the weather is warm because midget faded rattlesnakes (*Crotalus viridis concolor*) have been found in Spooky Gulch.

Follow the Hole-in-the-Rock Road for 26 miles. At the lone juniper on the right and the signed junction, make a left-hand turn. Make another left-hand turn and you'll be at the trailhead in 1.7 miles. This last section of the road is rutted and high clearance is recommended.

From the turnaround where you park your car, walk north to the edge and start down. Almost immediately there are several little stair steps in a natural crack that will get you below the ridge. Large cairns guide you on the route down. Follow the wide, sandy draw until it starts to drop sharply away. Work your way to the west side of the wash and drop down the sand dune until you're back in the wash. Stay in the wash until it intersects Dry Fork.

Exploring up-canyon, it immediately slots up. Walking in the wash, the walls stay constricted for about a half mile.

Down-canyon, Peek-a-boo is the first narrow opening coming in from the north. This is a good place to assess your climbing ability, both

Natural bridge, Peek-a-boo Canyon          Spooky Gulch

up and down. The hike description is written by going up this slot first. You can access the mouth of Spooky on the crossover route that can be used to climb the rock jam in Spooky from the bottom.

Climb up the cut steps to enter this delightful drainage. Negotiate the scooped-out pockets till you encounter a double natural bridge. Farther up this convoluted slot are two more small natural bridges. These carved-out features give this slot its name.

When you hit the first wide, sandy area, it's easier to go up and around on the right side. It's a serious squeeze for the next fifteen feet or so. Dropping back into Peek-a-boo it quickly becomes a sensuous passage again. When the walls fade away, it becomes a very wide, sandy wash.

Leave the sandy wash and head east for a half mile to enter Spooky Gulch from the top. It quickly walls up. There's a rock jam in the early portion that you negotiate for a six-foot descent. Next is a small natural bridge. You can crawl through the natural bridge or go around it. From here down, the passage progressively narrows. Most of the time it is necessary to walk sideways with your day pack in your hand. The walls

Author in Spooky Gulch

curve inward near the top, so only occasional light shafts filter down. Exiting Spooky Gulch, you have just experienced a great slot canyon.

At the mouth of Spooky, head down Dry Fork of Coyote to get to Brimstone. There is a chock stone blocking the narrow stretch a half mile up from the mouth of Brimstone Gulch. It can be climbed on either side. The lower mile of Brimstone is a very wide, open draw but it quickly narrows above the sand slide. It is very dark about a half mile up the narrows and a cold-looking pool stopped me. The walls widened just enough that I couldn't bridge across it. Walking the western rim above Brimstone, it remains very narrow for at least a mile.

Return up Dry Fork to your exit climb.

## HIKE 24: RED WELL

Difficulty: Moderate
Length (one way): 6 miles
Time: 1 day
Maps: Big Hollow Wash, King Mesa
Water: Coyote Gulch

Although not as popular as Hurricane Wash as a route to lower Coyote Gulch, this slightly longer hike (by 0.7 mile) is scenic and not as crowded. Wide benches are followed by a tight constriction. Several colorful side spurs add diversity. Campsites are numerous.

There is a BLM sign announcing the turn to the Red Well trailhead. This sign is 30.6 miles down the Hole-in-the-Rock Road. Taking the left fork, a trail register appears in 1.3 miles.

The name Red Well came from an early sheepherder by the name of Ersell ("Red") Shirts, who dug a well in the wash so that the sheep could have water. That actual location is south of this trailhead.

From the sign, pick up the path just to the north that immediately heads down to Big Hollow Wash. At this point it is a dry, sandy wash. A quick mile-and-a-half walk and Dry Fork of Coyote Wash enters from the left. There are wide, sandy benches above the stream with the sandstone walls off in the distance. The first side draw forces you down closer to the floor of the stream. Just before the next side spur drops in, there are two sets of narrows. It is easier to pass both on the south side. Exploration is best done without a pack.

The Park Service fence appears shortly after these challenges. The canyon starts to deepen and narrow and the colorful walls of Navajo sandstone are quite brown and tarnished.

The second fence is encountered after another mile of hiking. This fence is strategically located right after a short side slot and a bend in the stream.

After another half mile, water enters from a northern side arm. There's a pseudo-entrance before a domed rock but the real passage is just beyond. This narrow side canyon is loaded with willows so it is

Sideblotched lizard

a struggle heading up to explore. As you pass the dry waterfall on the right in about a half mile, there are two large overhangs in the bends of the canyon. Another half mile and the canyon boxes up.

Back down Coyote Gulch, small groves of juniper dot the bends of the stream. After another two miles of easy walking, the canyon widens and a large stand of cottonwoods covers the bench. Directly ahead is a dry overhang that has several level camp spots. Rainwater poured over the northern edge one night we were there and it sounded as though it was roaring through our bedroom.

Another narrow side slot enters from the north. A quarter-mile stroll up this arm will bring you to a grooved pour-off. One spring the pools along this canyon were filled with strings of frog eggs.

There is a short narrow passage. The next side canyon coming in from the west is Hurricane Wash.

Waterfall, Coyote Gulch

## HIKE 25: FOOLS CANYON

Difficulty: Strenuous
Length (one way): 8 to 14 miles
Time: 3 to 5 days
Water: Fools, Escalante River

This challenging hike has many rewards: solitude, slickrock vistas, a slot canyon, and dramatic views into Fools Canyon. The steep descent into Fools follows an old cattle route. The hike starts at the Red Well trailhead (HIKE 24).

There are two exits from Dry Fork Coyote Gulch to the overland route to Fools Canyon. The first is the vegetated, narrow side slot where Gulch is labeled on the topographic map. A big domed rock juts out just before this side drainage. It is a half-mile bushwhack to the break in the canyon wall on the east side. Climb up the small sand dune and then a short slickrock climb will get you up and out. Locate the shallow draw heading northeast. Stay on the south side and head in a northeasterly direction. I haven't explored this draw as it slots up.

The second route is just around the bend from this side drainage. It climbs directly up the slickrock and then around the shallow draw to the east. Continue north for half a mile until you intersect the previously mentioned draw heading northeast. Stay on the east side of this deepening slot. As it makes a final, gentle turn to the northeast, the saddle on the east end of King Mesa is your destination. Cresting the saddle, another drainage will bring you to the rim of Fools Canyon with views of its straight walls and sheer drop.

Contour east along the rim until you reach a promontory marking the first southeastern side canyon that prevents further easy travel to the east. This promontory of domed rocks on purple beds marks the route down an old cattle track. It drops along a crack in the Navajo sandstone, then zigzags down the Kayenta Formation to the canyon floor.

There are camp spots up-canyon. Exploring up-canyon, you may have to pass a water pocket on the north side. The canyon floor becomes purple beds. All of the branches dead-end.

Stream detail

Jacob Hamblin Arch, Coyote Gulch

Going down-canyon, the first camp spot is at the mouth of Fools Canyon. There is a worn path that stays above the cattails. When it rejoins streamside, a tricky crossing through the grass will take you up on a bench on the north side. When the path crosses the stream, walk in the stream bed till the pour-off. Climb sharply up the south side and stay on the bench for a quarter of a mile and a steep descent when the bench pinches out. Follow the drainage to the junction with the Escalante River.

## HIKE 26: HURRICANE WASH–COYOTE GULCH

Difficulty: Moderate
Length (one way): 13 miles
Time: 2 to 3 days
Maps: Big Hollow Wash, King Mesa, Stevens Canyon South
Water: Coyote Gulch

This is the easiest and shortest approach route to lower Coyote Gulch, the most popular hike in the area. A natural bridge, two arches, cascading waterfalls, deep overhangs, a sculptured streambed, and a rincon all add up to a very scenic canyon.

The trailhead is readily visible roughly 34 miles down the Hole-in-the-Rock Road as you pass the cabin and corral on the left side of the road. There is a large parking area on the right.

Heading down the open, sandy Hurricane Wash, this is no indication of the splendid canyon sights to follow. Several small constrictions alternate with a wide wash. The wash remains dry for almost four miles. By now the walls have attained some height.

A couple of sharp bends bring you to the national park fence. There is a hiker's maze to pass through. This arrangement prevents cattle from passing by and solves the problem of gates being left open. Please use it. From here the springtime greenery accompanies you to the junction with Coyote Gulch.

There is water flowing in this drainage, also. From here it is 7.9 miles to the Escalante River. There is a large, sandy bench across the

Coyote Natural Bridge

stream from the junction. This is the first of the many available campsites heading downstream.

After a couple of meanders, a small tributary comes in from the north (left). A short detour will add to your trip. When the alcove appears to the right, you can either continue at creek level or scramble up to the bench. Either route brings you to an amphitheater at the upper end, but the higher one gets you to the base of a dry waterfall.

As you continue down Coyote Gulch, water seeps start to appear along the walls near stream level. The bend before and the one after Jacob Hamblin Arch are deeply overhung, with desert varnish streaks giving you an idea of the vertical relief. It's a fish-eye view when you look up inside one of these bends. You can climb through the opening of this massive arch from either side. There is a pit toilet on the bench before Jacob Hamblin Arch and another one by Cliff Arch. Please use these as this canyon sees heavy usage.

The first really usable water seeps appear on the fern-covered bank just past the arch. You can stand in the creek and catch any of the several voluminous streams of water. A shallow overhang on the opposite bank makes a great place to camp. One spring when we camped at this spot, we were kept awake by the loud croaking of the frogs calling for a mate. Spring colors continue along the stream. The tall red paintbrush (*Castilleja chromosa*) blend well with the exposed rust-colored Kayenta beds over which the stream passes. These scooped-out pockets and narrow troughs first appear after four more bends.

The passageway constricts, then turns sharply through a narrow portal framed on the right by a rock pillar. The bend behind it is a rincon, a former meander of the stream.

One more bend brings you to Coyote Natural Bridge. The prevalence of coyotes in the whole region was the reason for the naming of the gulch and this natural bridge.

After you've gone another mile downstream, there appears to be a large domed rock blocking your path. There are two alternate routes available. If you look up to the cliff on the left, there appears to be an arch. This is actually just a dark hole.

Choice one goes up and over the saddle behind the rock dome. There is an excellent view of Cliff Arch from that saddle. Go left through the cottonwoods along the bank. There is a defined path up and to the right where the rock face is not smooth and sheer. After you start to descend on the other side of the ridge, there are some grooves cut into the sandstone to indicate the way. The trail winds toward the waterfall and then switches back the other direction, taking you back down to streamside.

The second choice is to stay along the water and follow it around the bend. At the far side of the domed rock, a rockfall has obstructed the channel. The first few blocks have to be bypassed. Then you cross to the right bank and locate the path that climbs up and around the worst part of the rock jam and the resultant waterfall. This trail stays high as it rounds the corner. There is another view of the arch. Directly below is a level, potential campsite. The trail slopes down and rejoins the stream.

Travel below this point becomes more challenging. You pass another rincon on the left. The first two waterfalls can be bypassed on the right side. After you pass the second one, you have to step down the purple ledges to reach the stream again.

Author's camp, Coyote Gulch

When the canyon turns east again just past the second waterfall, a thin waterfall comes off the north wall. A huge overhang that could sleep fifteen people greets you around the next bend.

You can carefully walk down the ledges at the edge of the next stair-step waterfall. The rate of descent appears quite steep through this half mile because the Navajo cliffs have risen high above you. This section has a profusion of seeps on the north wall.

Having gone through the wiggles of the "W" (that is what it looks like on the topographic map), the banks disappear and the walls close in. There is a side route that takes you up the Kayenta ledges as an alternate route to Stevens Canyon (HIKE 28). This bypass trail takes off on the left, from the downstream end of a bench with large cottonwood trees, some of which have been burned. It switches back and forth, leveling out and heading east around the neck of the promontory. To get a good view of Stevens Arch, leave the trail and walk toward the edge of that point. The route continues towards the north and heads down the first side draw to the river.

Continuing down Coyote Gulch, you reach the area of the rock jam in the streambed. Find the path on the right side that starts by a cottonwood tree and a big boulder. The Crack-in-the-Wall (HIKE 27) route climbs straight up the hillside at this point and goes between the rock domes visible to the south.

To continue down Coyote, carefully walk the sloped ledge until you can descend back to stream level. There may be logs placed against the wall to aid in the descent. An overhang against the north wall is a great camp spot. Another half mile brings you to the mouth of Coyote Gulch where it intersects the Escalante River.

## HIKE 27: FORTYMILE RIDGE–CRACK-IN-THE-WALL

Difficulty: Moderate
Length (one way): 2 miles
Time: 1/2 day
Maps: Sooner Bench, King Mesa, Stevens Canyon South
Water: Bring your own, Coyote Gulch

This route provides access to the Escalante River or lower Coyote Wash. It is an exposed, cross-country walk and not recommended for summertime hiking. There are outstanding views of the Henry Mountains in the distance and domed buttes near the mouth of Coyote Gulch. The narrow Crack-in-the-Wall is an interesting route off the rim. Bring a thirty-foot rope with which to lower packs.

The turn-off for this hike is 36 miles down the Hole-in-the-Rock Road. The trailhead parking for two-wheel-drive vehicles is left up the hill in 4.4 miles. There is a trail register there. The road shortly forks left and becomes four-wheel-drive with deep sand. A second trail register appears in another two miles.

From the trailhead, head down the ridge. Follow the sand down to the slickrock. Walk in a northeasterly direction until you hit the Crack-in-the-Wall. Cairns are not good indicators. You can look down on the southern end of the sand dune. If you have drifted too far south, you'll look down the cliffs at the Escalante River.

The crack is very narrow and runs parallel to the canyon wall. Lower your pack over the edge using that rope you brought with you. Maneuver sideways to get through. At the base of the crack, retrieve your pack and head down the sand dune. This will drop you into Lower Coyote Gulch. Go down-canyon to the Escalante River, then upstream to get to Stevens Canyon (HIKE 28).

To complete the loop hike exiting on the Jacob Hamblin route, hike up Coyote Gulch. The exit route starts on the south side just before the arch. It is a steep ascent up ridged sandstone, climbing over a hundred vertical feet. A safety belay at the top from an experienced rock climber is advisable.

When you have reached the canyon wall above Coyote Gulch, this description leads you to the first trailhead on Fortymile Ridge. Aim for the pile of dark brown boulders to the south that look like they've been dropped on top of the pinkish-orange sandstone. Hiking past the chocolate boulders, you'll see a gap between the orange dome and a dark red mesa. Climb through the pass and follow the white ledge to the right. Then head across the sand for a half mile and up the hill to the trail register.

The second route brings you to the trail register at the end of the Fortymile Ridge Road. Leaving the brown boulders described in the previous paragraph, contour southeast on the rolling domes of sandstone, staying below the top of slickrock. Head east for the farthest sandy, red-capped mesa until you hit the fence line. After crossing the fence, look for Stevens Arch to the east. Curve southeast and climb around the edge of the mesa. Head southeast across the blackbrush flats to the southern end of the next red-topped mesa that comes into view. When you top that rise, the trail register is visible. A little more sandy walking brings you to your vehicle.

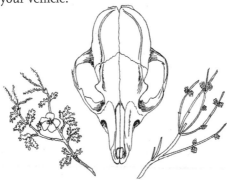

Author in Crack-in-the-Wall

Hiker on sand dune

## HIKE 28: STEVENS CANYON

Difficulty: Strenuous
Length (one way): 11 miles
Time: 4 days
Maps: King Mesa, Stevens Canyon South, Stevens Canyon North

This long canyon has plenty of challenges with scenery to match. A bit of work to get into, poison ivy, a natural bridge, and panoramic views at the second level, all make this a very special place to explore.

The easiest access is using the Crack-in-the-Wall route from the Fortymile Ridge trailhead (HIKE 27). After going down the sand dune and lower Coyote Gulch and hiking a mile up the Escalante River, the first opening on the right is Stevens Canyon.

When you come to the first pool, climb up the log jam on the left. You might want to haul your pack up after yourself. At the next pool, there is a rock pile to aid in the ascent. At the grotto, check out the natural bridge before climbing up the slippery, mossy wall. Watch out for poison ivy. Work your way through the boulders back to the canyon floor. There's a monstrous overhang on the north wall with high and low camp spots.

Continue up-canyon until you see the narrow overhang. The canyon floor is fluted in delightful patterns. Look right for the route, which goes up the rock slope until it levels out. Continue down-canyon to the bottom of the crack. Reverse and go up the slope to the top of the Wingate. The ledge walk will take you above and around the constriction in the canyon.

Contour the first draw on the right. The route stays at the same height. You can go down to the canyon floor but it ends in an impassable pour-over. When you pass the pour-over on the high route, descend the sand slope past the juniper tree to the canyon floor. Continue walking the canyon floor past impressive side forks as the canyon turns north. Pass through some narrows to where the ground around the bend is covered with vegetation due to a spring just upstream. There is a lot more of Stevens Canyon to explore.

## HIKE 29: DANCE HALL ROCK

Difficulty: Easy
Length (one way): 1/16 of a mile
Time: 1/2 hour
Map: Sooner Bench
Water: Bring your own

This historic outcropping of Entrada sandstone was used by the Hole-in-the-Rock expedition as a place to dance. The relatively smooth floor of the amphitheater made this a natural gathering spot. By climbing around the amphitheater, it is possible to explore the solution holes that have been weathered into the sandstone.

This historic site is also signed, 36.7 miles down the Hole-in-the-Rock Road. The parking area is just off the road, with Dance Hall Rock visible directly ahead. It is an easy walk from the parking spot up to the open area of Dance Hall Rock.

Dance Hall Rock

The San Juan Mission camped for three weeks near Fortymile Spring just to the south. Serious road work was required to get from here to Hole-in-the-Rock. As late arrivals joined the trek, the company spent some of their evenings dancing at this natural stage. There were three fiddlers plus other musicians, so they must have had a good time. With winter snow blocking the road back to Escalante, the decision was made to push on through the rugged country ahead.

There is plenty of open slickrock country to explore behind Dance Hall Rock. Careful friction walking up the sandstone slopes reveals an altered landscape. A variety of solution holes have been weathered into the sandstone. One of the deepest ones has enough soil in the bottom to contain a large cottonwood tree. Others have filled in with sand and vegetation and look like miniature desert gardens.

Grass, cottonwood, and slump block, Fortymile

Concretions

## HIKE 30: FORTYMILE GULCH

Difficulty: Strenuous
Length (one way): 6 miles
Time: 1 day
Maps: Sooner Bench, Davis Gulch
Water: Fortymile Gulch

This highly scenic route gets more challenging as it progresses. The varied terrain and ever deepening walls make this a colorful hike. This hike contains a wonderful surprise. All of the side washes of this drainage presented steep barriers to the San Juan expedition as they built their wagon road toward the Colorado River.

There is no sign marking this trailhead so careful attention needs to be paid to the mileage log for the Hole-in-the-Rock Road. Two miles past the sign to Fortymile Spring, 39.4 miles down the Hole-in-the-Rock Road,

Author in water pockets, side canyon of Fortymile

the road dips into Carcass Wash. The traffic accident monument is just up the hill. Park on the right. The name Carcass Wash was derived from cattle falling to their death when they tried to cross this narrow chasm. The Glen Canyon NRA boundary sign is a hundred feet down-canyon.

Head down the wash until you come to a gray pour-off. Stay on the bench on the south side for a quarter mile. Carefully work your way down the sandy slope until you get to the floor of the wash. It is an easy stroll for the next mile to the junction with Fortymile Gulch.

The gulch is still wide at this point although the canyon walls in the distance are getting higher. After another mile of travel, the narrow slot of Sooner Wash comes in on the right. This is an exciting side defile to explore without a pack. Some chimneying techniques are necessary for

Hidden waterfall, Fortymile

climbing over the numerous large boulders that block this wash. (This route is not recommended as an alternate route back to the trailhead because of the scrambling involved in getting over these chockstones and some challenging climbing at the upper end.)

Farther down Fortymile there are several dead-end short draws that come in from the north side. Water appears right after you've passed the second side draw. As you round the first bend after the water starts to flow, look for the portion of the cliff that has fallen away from the right wall. The route can either follow the stream or you can climb onto the large benches above the stream.

The stream angles to the north and it's time for another side excursion up the drainage heading due north. This easy walk has some finely

Dead-end side canyon, route to Broken Bow Arch

scooped-out water pockets where the erosional forces have been at work on an exposed sandstone slab. This side arm comes to an abrupt halt. The fluted pattern of this jump and the large, sandy amphitheater that end this walk were inducements for exploring every side drainage I passed.

The next bend brings the surprise—a hidden waterfall. There's a small camp spot at the top and an easy route down the sand on the right.

Another two bends and it's time to start wading. The walls have seriously closed in at this point. A short passage where the water slides over bedrock is followed by a chockstone and deep wading or a potential swim. Stemming (arms and feet on opposite walls as you maneuver above the pool) can get you through this first tight stricture but this technique is challenging with the weight of a pack. You'll walk in water under the wedged rock along the convoluted passage until its junction with Willow Gulch.

The entrance for the Fortymile-Willow loop starts at the Willow Gulch trailhead (HIKE 31).

## HIKE 31: WILLOW GULCH

Difficulty: Moderate
Length (one way): 3 miles
Time: 1 day
Maps: Sooner Bench, Davis Gulch
Water: Willow Gulch

This highly scenic, short hike has a very impressive arch that protrudes majestically away from the canyon wall. The nature of the canyon changes quickly in its short course, with a luxurious growth of spring flowers along the lower walls. This hike can be combined with Fortymile Gulch (HIKE 30) to make a challenging one- or two-day loop trip.

Turn left off of the Hole-in-the-Rock Road after 41.5 miles (276 blue stake sign) and follow this spur for 1.4 miles to the trail register.

Head down the sand dune past the tilted capped rock to the canyon floor. Before starting down-canyon, take a short walk up through the narrows. Just when it opens up, there is a hanging garden and cave on

Broken Bow Arch

the north wall. Hanging gardens are a characteristic feature of the region, and are formed where there is water seepage along the horizontal bedding planes of the sandstone rocks. Such water-loving plants as maidenhair fern (*Adiantum capillus-veneris*), golden columbine (*Aquilegia chrysantha*), and red monkey flowers (*Mimulus cardinalis*) usually can be found here.

Going down-canyon, bypass the narrows on the right (south) side. The short side spur coming in from the south can be explored until it dead ends in a dry fall. An overland route leads up the left arm. This will take you cross country, around the dome on the north side, and drop you into Willow Gulch in about a half a mile. The second choice is to continue down the wash for another half mile where it joins Willow Gulch.

Going up canyon, this wash is walkable all the way back to the Hole-in-the-Rock Road, but it loses character in a half mile. That first half mile is worth the exploration. There's a large alcove a quarter mile up on the east side that is a perfect spot to sit and relax.

The flow of water increases with the addition of the spring just below the fork. The water cascades over the layered red rocks of the Kayenta Formation.

The stream holds your attention until a massive arch looms up in front of you. In the class and style of Rainbow Natural Bridge, this large arm of sandstone projecting from the north wall is one of the scenic marvels of the lower Escalante Canyons. It was named Broken Bow Arch by local historian Edson B. Alvey because in 1930 he found an Indian bow underneath it. Photographers climb hills on either side of the canyon for a spectacular, well-balanced photograph. Another treat awaits the spring hikers as they walk the undercut banks of the bend beneath the arch. White, small-flowered columbine covers the seeps found there.

This gulch was named for the profusion of willows that grow along the banks. Here they add color and don't create a bushy jungle like those found along the main Escalante River.

Just before the union with Fortymile Gulch, the canyon walls close in and you'll be walking in water. The backed-up waters of Lake Powell Reservoir are downstream from this junction.

To do the Fortymile-Willow loop, head out cross-country from the trail register in a northwesterly direction until you hit the wash. Drop down just past the narrows and cross the wash. Head up the next north arm until you get to the top of the hill. Looking back, you can see the trailhead parking and Navajo Mountain in the background. Line them up. Now head up the green slope between the white-domed outcropping to the northeast and the small white cliff face. Head for the reddish dome

4326. Pass it on the left and head down the purple slickrock slope to the northwest. You can see the entrenched meander and dome 4141. The first route is down a steep friction walk just before the pour-off to the left. The easier route is to go around that pour-off and drop down the shelf with the chipped steps before the cairn at the rim. Fortymile Gulch is just down the wash.

## HIKE 32: FIFTYMILE CREEK

Difficulty: Moderate
Length (one way): 4 miles
Time: 1 day
Maps: Sooner Bench, Davis Gulch
Water: Lower Fiftymile Creek

Although the lower portion of the canyon and Gregory Natural Bridge are under the waters of Lake Powell, the remaining canyon is a quiet retreat. A skyline arch next to an overhang and a convoluted walk in the lower canyon are highlights.

This is another hike that starts at a side fork instead of at the head of the named canyon. Pull off to the right in the wash 45.5 miles down the Hole-in-the-Rock Road. Behind you is Cave Point, a projection of Fiftymile Mountain. Head down the boulder-strewn wash. The southern arm comes in shortly. Just as the walls start to attain some height, there is an abrupt drop. Climb up the bench on the north side. Once on the benchland, go around the first rise on the right, cross the fence, and skirt the second hill. On the other side there is a friction walk down to a sandy bench. This leads to a short descent to the canyon bottom.

Once on the canyon floor, there is time to observe the patterns of desert varnish on the canyon walls. The bushes with the spiny holly leaves are Fremont barberry. The sudden, loud whirl of a sage grouse (*Centrocercus urophasianus*) flying away is a heart stopper.

After two miles, the Fiftymile Creek drainage comes in from the right. Continuing downstream after the junction, ground water and cottonwood trees appear. A mile below the junction, a prominent overhang is a

Fiftymile Canyon

beckoning campsite. The sky was so dark and this shelter was so welcome that I didn't see the skyline arch until the following morning. If shelter is not essential, there are plenty of campsites on the sandy benchland.

A short climb up the draw coming in from the north is rewarding. The sculpturing effects of water are a constant eye catcher. There was

 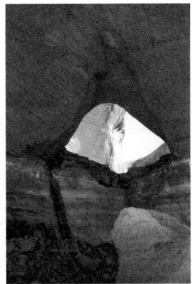

Fiftymile waterfall    La Gorce Arch

a Mexican free-tailed bat (*Tadarida brasiliensis*) with a broken wing next to the stream. Bats unfortunately evoke images of vampires. I'm glad to see them darting around my campsite since each swoop means one less insect to torment me. Their specialized ability to navigate using echolocation makes it possible to hunt at night. The information received from their emitted supersonic sounds accurately allows them to capture small insects on the wing.

All along the canyon there is evidence of beaver, from the gnawed-through cottonwood trees to the marks of the branches being dragged along the sand. Beaver found in the Colorado River and its tributaries do not build domed stick homes or dams. They have adapted to the seasonal fluctuations of water by digging holes in the banks.

After a rocky streambed and paths cutting the sandy benches, the pour-over appears. Below the pour-over, the narrows begin. This constricted, winding journey leads you from bend to bend until it hits the lake. This part of the canyon is a sharp contrast to the earlier feel of this hike. I seem to do this hike only when it's storming, so I witnessed cascading waterfalls on my last trip.

## HIKE 33: DAVIS GULCH

Difficulty: Strenuous
Length (one way): 5 miles
Time: 1 day
Map: Davis Gulch
Water: Davis Gulch

This canyon is the site of the mysterious disappearance of the young artist Everett Ruess. Davis Gulch has many attractions, among them a challenging overland approach, a steep stock trail as the entrance to the canyon floor, and a one-hundred-foot arch. The remoteness of the country, a deep narrow gash in the earth, and lost Indian ruins and petroglyphs add to the romance of this canyon. Everett said in his last letter: "Often as I wander, there are dream-like tinges when life seems impossibly strange and unreal."

Fifty miles down the Hole-in-the-Rock Road there is a short spur track to the right. Park there and hike back up the road. Leave the road at the second draw and head north out of the wash just after the junction with the wash coming in on the right. Head for the small red knoll that will shortly become visible. Drop off the northwest side and head north toward knoll 4321 across the open grassland. Then travel northeast, aiming just to the left of knob 4291.

Stay on the same level as much as possible for the next three and a half miles of cross-country travel. After wandering within the confines of canyon walls for years, there is a special feeling of freedom that comes from cross-country slickrock rambling.

At the first real break in the vertical walls, look east at the flat mesa top across the gulch and you will see a vertical cleft in the hillside. There are several rock cairns which warn you of the impending trail down. This is a stock trail used to bring cattle into the canyon. Follow along the side of the shallow depression until you're on the slickrock again. Locate the next rock cairn slightly to the right. If you lose the zigzag route and go too far northeast, you can look down to where logs are piled close to the

Author at entrance to Davis Canyon

base of the cliff. That is the end of the stock trail. There are steps cut in the rock just before the bottom.

Once you are on the canyon floor there is a well-worn path leading down-canyon. Camp spots abound. Lake Powell will be several bends downstream, depending on the lake level. In 2004 when the lake was low, I was able to hike to La Gorce Arch, named for Dr. John Oliver La Gorce, editor of the *National Geographic* magazine. A lot of history is buried under the waters of Lake Powell.

Davis Gulch was the last known campsite of the young artist Everett Ruess. His burros were found but his body and outfit were never recovered. This occurred in the fall of 1934, when Everett was just twenty-one years old. Everett had been exploring the southwest for several years, sketching, making block prints, and writing poetry. His disappearance remains a mystery and continues to draw modern-day attention.

Everett Ruess's thoughts help generate a sense of balance. Just a couple of short quotes from that other wanderer: "The wild silences have enfolded me, unresisting," and "I, too, am singing in my heart, and I sing the song of the wilderness."

Heading up-canyon, the canyon is very brushy and filled with beaver ponds. Bement Arch leaps out at you from the north wall. Climb up the rubble and, from inside, it will appear even more massive. Named during the same National Geographic exploration of "Escalante: Utah's River of Arches" in 1955, Harlon Bement was the Utah state aeronautics director and an avid aerial explorer.

If you continue upstream, the water stops flowing and Davis Gulch becomes a sandy wash. The hike ends at a pour-off. Davis Gulch from the road is a challenging canyoneering route.

## HIKE 34: HOLE-IN-THE-ROCK

Difficulty: Moderate
Length (one way): 1/4 mile
Time: 1/2 day
Map: Davis Gulch
Water: Bring your own

Although the bottom two-thirds of the original route has been flooded by Lake Powell, the upper third remains. This was the most challenging section, with remnants of the construction still visible. This site recognizes the important role pioneer determination played in early Mormon colonization. There is an excellent view of Cottonwood Canyon across the lake.

After the road crosses the head of Davis Gulch, it is four-wheel-drive for the next 5.5 miles. From the parking area at the end of the road, go east to find the commemorative plaque bolted into the sandstone. The route down starts in the notch immediately to the south. Rockfalls have made the passage more interesting, but they do not create any real barriers. A short way down, steps have been cut into the sandstone. They are believed to have been cut by miners in later years. The next section is Uncle Ben's Dugway. Besides cutting steps and creating a shelf, holes were drilled lower down and parallel to the shelf. Stakes were driven into these holes; logs and brush were piled up to provide a track for the outside wheels. The wagons were then safely taken down this improvised road.

Hole-in-the-Rock

From the bottom of the dugway, it is a gradual descent to the lake. When you get to the water's edge, look back up at the route taken in 1880 by 250 people and 80 wagons. The amazing thing is this portion of the trek was considerably easier than some of the obstacles encountered on the east side of the river.

Andrew P. Schow and Reuben Collet had explored the country southeast of Escalante and took "an improvised two-wheeled cart" down the Hole-in-the-Rock. These early Escalante settlers played an important role in determining the route taken by the San Juan Mission.

The primary reason for the San Juan Mission was to establish better relations with the Indians. Converts from the southern states were also looking for a place to live that had a warmer winter climate than their settlement in Colorado. The Mormon Church also wanted settlers to inhabit the borderland as a buffer against encroachment by stockmen from Colorado.

The whole expedition was on the move for six months. It took a month and a half to enlarge the original Hole-in-the-Rock and construct a road three-quarters of a mile down to the Colorado River. When they finally reached the San Juan River, just east of Cottonwood Wash, they were just eighteen miles from their intended destination at Montezuma, but they were too exhausted to continue. The site they settled is now known as Bluff. This incredible journey remains a milestone in the annals of western settlement.

This route was used for another year as the main road between the two settlements. Charles Hall operated the ferry at the Hole-in-the-Rock crossing for the rest of 1880, when the lack of traffic caused him to move to a more favorable site at the mouth of Hall's Creek.

**9**

# Hell's Backbone

## Map, Road Log, Hikes

This highly scenic road, built by the CCC in the 1930s, connected Escalante and Boulder. Winding through the forest, there are excellent views of the slickrock country. The Hell's Backbone Bridge crosses a small saddle between two canyons of colorful sandstone. The aspen add additional color in the fall. For the hiker, this road provides access to some of the most challenging hiking found in the area.

| MILES | | DESCRIPTION |
|---|---|---|
| From Escalante | From Boulder | |
| 0.0 | 41.0 | Escalante Visitor Center |
| 1.3 | 39.7 | Turn left for Hell's Backbone Road |
| 1.8 | 39.2 | Escalante River crossing |
| 8.9 | 32.1 | Turnoff to the Box (R). This is the exit for Pine Creek **(HIKE 35)**. |
| 15.2 | 25.8 | Turnoff (L) to Posey Lake and Loa |
| | | 1.3   Hog Spring Ranch Road (L) |
| | | 2.1   Posey Lake Campground (L) |
| | | **HIKE 36: POSEY LAKE LOOKOUT** |
| 19.2 | 21.8 | CCC Plaque (L). Civilian Conservation Corps history |
| 19.7 | 21.3 | **HIKE 35: PINE CREEK:** The Box |
| 19.9 | 21.1 | Turnoff (L) to Blue Spruce Campground |
| | | 0.5   Blue Spruce Campground |
| | | 0.8   Cowpuncher Guard Station |
| | | 1.6   Unnamed road (L) |
| | | 1.8   **HIKE 37: JACOB'S RESERVOIR** |
| 23.3 | 17.8 | Unnamed road (L). Go straight. |

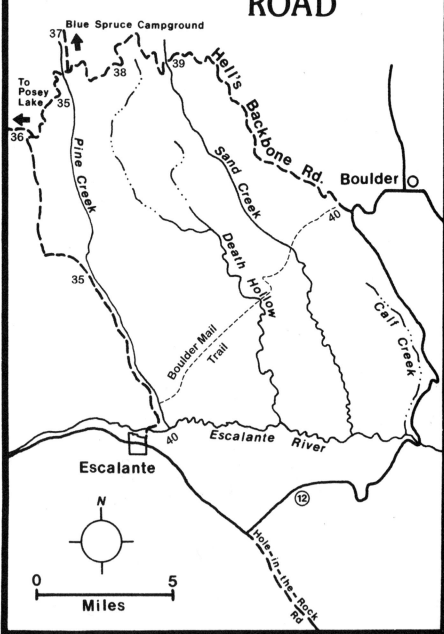

| | | |
|---|---|---|
| 25.0 | 16.0 | **HIKE 38: DEATH HOLLOW**–Trailhead (L) |
| 26.3 | 14.7 | Hell's Backbone Bridge. When the CCC built this road in the 1930s, the crew working from the east had made the bridge so it would be ready when the two crews met. The views are spectacular. The road is narrow as you head down. Rocky mountain juniper, with its droopy branches, and the colorful red-barked manzanita line the road. |
| 29.2 | 11.8 | **HIKE 39: SAND CREEK** |
| 39.7 | 1.3 | Big Hollow |
| 40.8 | 0.2 | Unnamed road (R) crosses Boulder air strip. |
| | | **HIKE 40: BOULDER MAIL TRAIL** |
| 41.0 | 0.0 | Highway 12  Turn left to go to Boulder and right to Escalante. |

## HIKE 35: PINE CREEK–THE BOX

Difficulty: Moderate
Length (one way): 8 miles
Time: 1 day
Maps: Posey Lake, Wide Hollow Reservoir
Water: Pine Creek

This is a delightful day stroll down a stream. The area known as the Box has high, multicolored sandstone walls which contrast sharply with the dark green of the ponderosa pine trees. The route requires several stream crossings, but these are generally easy. There are pools for soaking and broad sandy benches for camping.

Drive north out of Escalante, using the Hell's Backbone road log for mileage. The starting point is a small pullout at mile 19.7. The pullout is on the right-hand side of the road next to a Forest Service sign that closes the area behind the sign to vehicles. If you are only going to take a short hike and explore the lower portion of Pine Creek, there is a small Forest Service sign 8.9 miles north of Escalante directing you to a small parking area. Follow the dirt road to the Box.

From the pullout on the east side of the road, head straight down the hillside to creek level. In a quarter mile, cross back to the west side where Blue Spring Creek enters. A short walk up this stream will reward you with a view of a waterfall. Continuing down Pine Creek, the banks of the next mile are crowded with wild rose plants (*Rosa woodsii*). Careful route selection or long pants make travel through this section easier. The next challenge is a recent rockfall on the west bank. After you negotiate your way through the fallen trees, the walking becomes easier.

In another mile the canyon opens up on the east side and the sharp relief of the Navajo sandstone cliffs holds the eye. The red bark of the manzanita (*Arctostaphylos pungens*) shrubs contrasts majestically against the white sand. Geraniums, evening primroses, paintbrushes, skyrockets, and DYCs dot the landscape. (A "DYC" is a darn yellow composite, part of the largest family of flowering plants and difficult to correctly identify.)

Pine Creek

The sandy benches contain stands of tall ponderosa pine (*Pinus ponderosa*) trees, easily recognizable with their sets of three long needles. The scales of the bark of this tree resemble a bird or anything else you can imagine. It can grow to tremendous proportions, especially along the wetter Pacific Coast. The name ponderosa was suggested by David Douglass, the Scottish explorer of the Northwest. The seeds were eaten raw or made into bread by the Indians. Squirrels, chipmunks, and birds also enjoy the seeds.

After about another mile, Deep Creek comes in from the west. This creek can be used as a loop route if transportation hasn't been arranged at the mouth of the Box. This side drainage is well named because the banks are steep. It is easier to walk on the north hillside above the stream. There is a delicate waterfall in this drainage.

The red stalk with the cluster of whitish, bell-like flowers found near the mouth of Deep Creek is a species that cannot manufacture its own food. Woodland pinedrops (*Pterospora andromedea*), part of the Heather family, utilizes the food made by the fungi that decay fallen plant material.

Heading down-canyon, the next half mile is more intimate. The path is closer to the stream and the sandstone walls crowd the creek bank. When side drainages appear on the east side, the Box opens up and presents a display of crossbedded, multitiered sandstone walls. After the next stream crossing, the path remains on the east bank for a while. In most places there is a passageway on either bank and you can choose the number of stream crossings. There are three types of crossings: walking across fallen tree trunks, boulder hopping, or wading.

At the first large promontory on the east bank that forces the stream to bend, the path follows the streambed. At the next outcropping, the route goes over the back side of the sandstone wedge. The sandy benches provide ample campsites. The final mile is twisty as the stream turns southwest and cuts its way through the Escalante Monocline. There is a fence in one of the constricted bends, then one or two more water crossings and you're out of the Box.

## HIKE 36: POSEY LAKE LOOKOUT

Difficulty: Easy
Length (one way): 1/2 mile
Time: 1 hour
Maps: Posey Lake
Water: At the campground

This short, four-hundred-foot uphill walk takes you to an overlook that offers a wide vista. The profusion of wildflowers along the way turns this into a nature walk. This is bear habitat so be aware.

Head up the Hell's Backbone Road for 15.2 miles to the Posey Lake junction. Two miles on this road takes you to the campground. The signed trail starts next to campsite no. 14.

A short, steep climb takes you around the hill and up to a small, roofed platform. To the east, the sandstone cliffs of Pine Creek stand out in bold relief against the spruce and pine forest. Farther east, the Henry Mountains captivate the skyline. (These laccolithic mountains were first described by Grove Karl Gilbert of the then newly formed U.S. Geological Survey. Laccoliths are dome-shaped intrusive structures. In a modern re-examination of the Henrys, Charles Hunt concluded that the laccoliths were fed by a central stock that intruded up through the overlaying sedimentary rocks. This configuration of a central stock and spreading laccolithic branches resembles cacti with arms. These isolated mountains, named the Dirty Devil Mountains by A. H. Thompson, were discovered in 1872 by members of the second Powell expedition when they traveled overland to retrieve a boat left at the mouth of the Dirty Devil River.

On a clear day, the Abajo or Blue Mountains can be seen farther east. Navajo Mountain, also a laccolith, stands alone to the south. This peak is sacred to the Navajo Indians.

Wandbloom penstemon (*Penstemon virgatus*) is a pale-violet flower found along the trail. This flower is unique in that the tongue-like stamen is not hairy like in the rest of the penstemons. The Gambel oak, a low shrub, is also much in evidence. William Gambel was a young

Sego lilies

ornithologist who came out west with Thomas Nuttal in 1844. He discovered about a hundred new species but the rigors of frontier life did not agree with him. Succumbing to typhoid after a winter crossing of the Nevada desert and the Sierra Nevada Mountains, he was buried at Rose's Bar, California. Not even his bones found any rest because they were sluiced down the hillside when the forty-niners discovered hydraulic mining. The acorns of the oak named after him are avidly eaten by wild turkeys and squirrels while mule deer browse the green foliage.

Returning from the lookout, a short side trip down the west slope of the hill brings you to a shallow green area. Continue along the open area to the south and the first of the Tule Lakes comes into view. These shallow ponds are duck havens. Return by the same route to the trail.

The chattering noise coming from the trees belongs to the spruce squirrel (*Tamiasciurus hudsonicus fremonti*). You are made well aware of the fact that you have entered this small animal's territory. The short tail and black stripe on its side are distinctive. These energetic workers help perpetuate the forests by storing pine cones in the soil.

## HIKE 37: JACOB'S RESERVOIR

Difficulty: Strenuous
Length (one way): 5.4 miles
Time: 1 day
Maps: Big Lake, Jacob's Reservoir
Water: Pine Creek

This trail is an excellent combination of hiking through the woods and high alpine meadows. A variety of wildlife can be spotted on this hike. This long drainage goes through quite a transformation before it joins the Escalante River. The Thompson party went up this stream to circumvent the canyons of the Escalante.

Take the Hell's Backbone Road north for 19.9 miles to the Blue Spruce Campground turnoff. Go past the campground for another 1.8 miles and pull off to the left by the Forest Service sign. The route follows an old pack trail and immediately crosses Pine Creek. At the end of the first open meadow, there is an old wooden tent structure. The route going up the hill to the right is signed Jubilee G.S. No. 24. This is the way to Jacob's Reservoir. The route contours around the hill, crossing several small streams. The bridged one is Pine Creek.

After continuing around the hill, the route seems to run out. Look uphill where the route picks up again, zigging and climbing steeply along the side of the hill. Going through the trees, the route finally levels off.

When the trail and Pine Creek join together again, the stream is bounded by rock outcroppings. This constriction is utilized by the cattlemen to divide grazing areas. Be sure to close the gate after passing through. The trail runs briefly alongside the water and then crosses it. Now it climbs up to a saddle. Here you are greeted by two large, built-up rock pillars: the one on the left has a telephone pole held in place by the rocks. The line ran from the Jubilee Guard Station (built in 1905 and restored in 1989), which is the rustic cabin just left of the trail. A new shingled roof offsets the darker cabin walls.

The route climbs sharply until it opens up into a boulder-strewn meadow. In late summer there is a chance of seeing mule deer grazing among the cows. The cairned way leads into the meadow and then turns sharply southeast until you see Pine Creek. Now the route turns northeast and runs along the creek until you can see Barney Lake against the talus slope. Continue along the west bank of Pine Creek until there is a small rise. The cairns lead you over the rise and away from the creek. Continue through the meadow to the next rise. You are now over 10,000 feet in elevation.

This is the dam of Jacob's Reservoir, where a yellow-bellied marmot has made a home among the boulders of the dam. The name *marmota* comes from the Dutch name of the European species of woodchuck. This ground-dwelling mammal is the largest rodent native to the Southwest. This animal occupies a tremendous altitude range and is found from the ponderosa pine community to above timberline. Its loud warning whistle is a familiar sound in these high meadows. It hibernates through the long winter months. Retrace your steps for the downhill return.

## HIKE 38: DEATH HOLLOW

Difficulty: Strenuous
Length (one way): 22.5 miles
Time: 4 days
Maps: Roger Peak, Escalante
Water: Death Hollow

This is the most challenging hike described in this book. The beautiful canyon has plenty of contrasts. There is no water in the upper section and then it becomes a canyoneering trip, negotiating drop-offs and swimming deep pools. There is poison ivy (*Taxicodendron radicans*) along the streambed, especially in the section traversed by the Boulder Mail Trail (HIKE 40).

Death Hollow

Before you start on this adventure, make sure that you are physically and mentally prepared. Protect your gear in waterproof containers. Bring emergency warm clothes to offset potential hypothermia. Make sure of the weather before you go, as threatening storms could produce flash floods. Conditions change so be prepared.

Go up the Hell's Backbone Road for 25 miles to the signed trailhead on the left side of the road. The descent is a gradual slope. Once you are on the floor of the drainage, the walk is a gentle stroll down a sandy wash. Towering Navajo cross-striated sandstone cliffs form the backdrop. Tall ponderosa pine trees add green and yellow hues.

After four miles or so an eastern arm runs closely parallel. There is only a small rise separating the two drainages. The canyon narrows after a while, but the same motif of sandy floor and white walls continues. This general impression of white is what remains in the memory of this upper section.

The variability of conditions at different times of the year and the effects of recent flash floods all influence the situation that you encounter next. The winter of 1983 was extremely dry, so early spring trips the following year were easy but dry. The pools were filled with sand and areas that normally require swimming were easily negotiated. Several years ago, all the pools were scoured out and full of water, requiring tremendous effort to negotiate.

It is possible to walk on the sandstone edge around the first of several pools created by chockstones blocking the streambed, but the walls quickly become too steep and a central route through the pools becomes necessary.

Some of the barrier stones are easy to scramble over, while others require a jump into the water below.

The last several pools were covered with floating debris and again we found a way around them.

When the chockstones and pools end, you are able to take the time to look around and appreciate the dynamic quality of the surrounding sandstone. As the stream mellows the small waterfalls, contrasting white and black patterns on the walls, and the increased green streamside vegetation all come together for a better feeling of what this canyon has to offer.

Note the spurter spring gushing several inches out of the ground on the south side. The vegetation makes it a challenge to cross from one side of the stream to the other. When the canyon continues in an easterly direction for a while, look for the telephone line spanning the canyon. The large cave on the northern wall is another indicator. This is where the Boulder Mail Trail comes down from Slickrock Saddle Bench.

Although there are numerous stream crossings in the next three miles, continued use has worn a path along the sandy benches. Several perpendicular, narrow slots take off on the east wall. The large bench and rocky western wall are part of the original Boulder Mail route. Rockfalls that made horse travel impossible ended travel out of Death Hollow at this point.

Around the next bend the canyon narrows again. This section has lots of ledges, and it may be possible to skirt some of the pools. Now there are some serious bends in the stream as the canyon works its way around some large, protruding blocks of sandstone. Walking is easy from here on out, either on sandy banks next to the stream or on the shallow bedrock.

There's a tremendous overhang cut under the dry waterfall coming in high on the western wall. Poison ivy is much in evidence in the greenery below the overhang. Another mile of walking brings you to the junction with the Escalante River. If you turn upstream at this point, it is 7.5 miles up the Escalante River (HIKE 2) to the trailhead. If you head downstream, it's 7.5 miles to Highway 12.

## HIKE 39: SAND CREEK

Difficulty: Strenuous
Length (one way): 20.5 miles
Time: 3 to 4 days
Maps: Roger Peak, Escalante, Calf Creek
Water: Sand Creek

This generally narrow canyon offers an adventure for well-prepared backpackers. Starting as a mountain stream that drains part of the Aquarius Plateau, it winds its way through slickrock benches to the Escalante River. The name was derived from those sandy formations, but it is often an apt description of the water. Brush and boulders make progress difficult, but solitude and exemplary scenery make this trip well worth the effort.

Follow the Hell's Backbone Road northeast out of Escalante for 29.2 miles to the Forest Service sign for Sand Creek. Start down the stream where it crosses the road. There is plenty of room to pull off the road on the east side of Sand Creek. Fendler rose (*Rosa fendleri*) and its stickers greet you right away. The fruits of this plant are the edible and highly nutritious rose hips, containing large amounts of vitamins A and C. They also provide food for a variety of animals and birds. Concentrated patches present a hindrance to travel.

In the first half mile, Grimes Creek and an unnamed little tributary add their flows to Sand Creek. When the walls start to close in, it's easier to traverse the sandy slopes above the creek. The banks become quite steep.

There are innumerable small waterfalls along the way, varying from one to two feet high. They are caused by boulders blocking the stream or trees that have fallen across. The channel remains very narrow, and when there are sandy benches, they are covered by manzanita and wild rose bushes. A recent flash flood had uprooted many trees and further blocked the passage, making this first part of the trip a serious endurance test.

There is a rapid drop in elevation as this stream steadily cuts down through the sandstone cliffs. Having left the blue spruce (*Picea pungens*) trees behind near the trailhead, ponderosa pine and Douglas

Sand Creek wall stain

fir (*Psuedotsuga menziesii*) cover the sandy slopes. The Douglas fir cone is distinctive because it has "mouse-tails" sticking out from between the cone scales. It is not a true fir, because its cones hang down and they fall off whole. A coffee substitute used to be made from the needles and twigs. The state tree of Oregon, it is a valuable lumber tree in the northwest.

The first western tributary is a narrow slit in the sandstone, ending quickly in a twenty-foot dry waterfall. The narrow channel continues to wind its way southeast. Rocky Mountain juniper (*Juniperus scopulorum*) and red-osier dogwood (*Cornus sericea*) are found at streamside. The bright red bark makes this an easy plant to identify. The pliable stems resemble the osier (willow) and were used in making baskets.

The first really good spots to camp occur when the canyon widens around the entrance of the first eastern tributary. It takes five hours to get to this point. The canyon quickly narrows again after this bend. The convoluted passage is broken by a series of narrow openings to the west. They don't go far before they pinch out.

All of a sudden an opening appears in the skyline and the high sandstone walls recede. You enter a broad, open valley with cottonwood trees along the stream and Utah juniper (*Juniperus osteosperma*) on the sloping hillsides. Campsites are plentiful. For the next two miles there are cattle paths on the benchland that can be followed. The rock layers are mudstones and shales that range from white to pinkish red. The banks are lined with willow shoots and beaver tracks.

Going on, the Navajo sandstone appears again and the canyon narrows but there is still plenty of walking room. Right after the western side slot, you pass a small grove of Gambel oak (*Quercus gambelii*) and several scooped-out pools as the creek cuts through bedrock. The benches are covered with gray rabbitbrush (*Ericameria nauseosus*). The light grayish green stalks of this tall bush are an aid in identification.

When the canyon opens up again there is a display of sandstone pillars and balancing rocks. There is an easy route on the eastern bank. The mouth of the next western tributary is barely discernable because of the heavy plant growth at its mouth.

A half mile or so before Sweetwater Creek enters, the Boynton Road crosses Sand Creek. This road was built to give easier access between

Boynton Road

Escalante and the scattered ranches in Salt Gulch. Very little evidence of this early 1900s road is left, since heavy rains washed out portions shortly after it was built.

The indication that Sweetwater Creek is close by occurs when a walkable ledge appears on the west bank. When this terrace slopes down, cross the stream and continue the journey on the eastern ledge.

At the dry hollow entering from the east, several large, volcanic rock cairns should be visible. These mark the Boulder Mail Trail, used to carry mail between Escalante and Boulder in the early 1900s.

It's time to thrash through the willows again. The large boulders in the stream make for slippery, treacherous crossings. There are several long, constricted areas where wading or swimming is required. In one pool, the water came right to my chin. It's tricky to negotiate those narrows because the silt gets stirred up so it's impossible to see the slippery, sloping walls underwater.

The streamside vegetation crowds in again when there is room to walk on the banks. The tall plants with clusters of purple flowers is common milkweed (*Asclepias speciosa*). The stems become fibrous as they get older, yielding a strong fiber that the Indians used for cordage.

Willow Patch Creek

The canyon country is in a constant state of flux. One year there are serious rockfalls, another year they are washed away. So a pool that had formed behind the rockfall is now gone. The narrow eastern side slot has a water seep. One small-flowered columbine (*Aquilegia micrantha*) was growing near the seep. Its deep violet and yellow colors made this flower very conspicuous.

The canyon is easier to negotiate a mile or so above Willow Patch Creek, with deepening walls replacing the heavy brush. There is a stand of oak trees that makes for a scenic camp spot on the high northern sand bench where the canyon really widens. Sagebrush (*Artemesia tridentata*) covers the wide, flat benchland.

A wandering garter snake (*Thamnophis elegans vagrans*) was spotted along the stream. This fast, nonvenomous snake has a distinct dorsal stripe and separate dark blotches. For the next mile, willow thickets crowd the stream and progress is slow.

Sand Hollow forms a dry waterfall just before it joins Sand Creek. The walking becomes easier as there is a path to follow and the vegetation is not as thick. The walls are high above as the stream winds along the last two miles. There is a spring at the wide, sandy mouth of Sand Creek.

Three miles of travel down the Escalante River (HIKE 2) brings you to the junction with Calf Creek and Highway 12.

## HIKE 40: BOULDER MAIL TRAIL

Difficulty: Strenuous
Length (one way): 16 miles
Time: 2 to 3 days
Maps: Boulder Town, Calf Creek, Escalante
Water: Sand Creek, Death Hollow. Seasonal water pockets may be found in Mamie Creek and on Antone Flat.

This popular route has seen increased use over the years so there is a discernable way for most of the route. There is still plenty of sand and slickrock to negotiate. This route has expansive vistas, outstanding opportunities for untrammeled wilderness exploration, and challenging slickrock hiking. The route is an important part of the early history of Escalante and Boulder.

Take Highway 12 east of Escalante for 25.7 miles. Turn left on the Hell's Backbone Road for 0.2 mile. The first left takes you 0.2 mile across the Boulder airstrip to the trailhead. If this road is too rocky, there is a small pullout at its start.

The route leads you through the trees and sagebrush until it finds the canyon wall. Dropping down the sandstone, you'll pass a juniper drift fence. Cairns mark the route down the slickrock to the floor of the wash that takes you to Sand Creek.

Cross the creek on the dark volcanic boulders that make convenient stepping stones. Then walk downstream along the west side of the creek. When the stream crowds against the western wall, a cairn marks the spot to head uphill. Contour around the hill, following the path that leads you to the dry drainage coming in on the right. Continue south until you see the cairn indicating the climb out of Sand Creek.

Starting in 1902, this route was traveled on a biweekly basis by postal riders. Before this time, mail delivery to Boulder had been sporadic. Mules were used to carry packages and supplies. In 1924, cans of cream also

Boulder airport

were shipped by this method, destined for the creamery at Osiris. This was the preferred summer route because it was about ten miles shorter than the Boulder road, which Utah 12 generally follows.

As you are struggling up the slickrock, you can see a butte on the horizon. The route heads around the right side of this butte. The cairned way heads up on the back side of the butte. The dry drainage you recently crossed is visible below you. Continue on the cairned route in a southwesterly direction toward a break in the Slickrock Saddle Bench. Spectacular views of Boulder Mountain, the Henry Mountains, and McGath Point are visible to the east. A portion of the old telephone line is present.

This line is part of the old Forest Service telephone system, established in 1910. It serviced thirty-five families in the Boulder area. Reeves

Baker, a long-time Escalante resident, interviewed by Rex Welles of the BLM, had the following comments to make about the system:

> Well, if you wanted me they'd ring two short ones and a long one. If they wanted my neighbor they'd ring maybe two long ones and a short, but everyone had his individual ring, and if you wanted to talk to your neighbor you had to know what his ring was, you just ring it, whatever his ring was, that was the way they did, and then if they wanted to talk over here [Escalante], they'd call Shurtz and he had a switchboard there where he'd connect you with the family you

Boulder mail trail                    Mamie Natural Bridge

wanted in Escalante, or anywhere as far as that goes. It was quite a phone line too. It was made up of bailing wire and small scraps of barbed wire. If you wanted to fix the line and you didn't have any phone wire you'd pick up a piece of barbed wire and put it in the gap. It was just a patched up affair.

Now the route brings you to the edge of Death Hollow. Follow the slickrock down to the tree, then turn and continue down the sloping ledge. Evidence remains of trail work for the passage of the horses. Note the huge alcove across the way as you continue to zigzag down to stream level.

The descent into Death Hollow is a steep, seven-hundred-foot drop. It was named because a pack animal fell to its death in the gorge. There are good camping spots after crossing the creek. The route down-canyon is lined with box elder (*Acer negundo*). The brown, dried-up leaves cling to your clothing when you pass by. There is poison ivy in profusion.

After six bends going downstream, or about a half mile, you'll come to a bend going to the right. There is a lone, tall, dead ponderosa pine trunk on the right bank. Look for the cairn at eye level. The cairned route takes you up the slickrock. When the juniper trees appear, cairns guide you around the west end of that north-facing escarpment. From the top of the ridge, head southwest. Juniper trunks that held the phone line are along the route. The way crosses sagebrush flats and open sandstone country.

Approaching Mamie Creek, the route goes to the right of the rock promontory. A steep descent is cairned down to the floor of Mamie Creek. Head down the sandy wash until you come to a pour-over and deep pool. Cairns to the right at the top of this drop lead you up and out of the wash. When you've located the route out, put down your pack and take a short side hike.

A mile walk down the wash will bring you to one of those secret delights of canyon exploration. Not marked on the topographic map is a thirty-foot-high natural bridge that surprises you shortly after rounding a sharp bend. This is followed by an abrupt pour-off. There is an urge in canyon country to go just one more bend and in this case the reward is a grand display.

The climb out of Mamie Creek is in a southwesterly direction, skirting both rock promontories on the right. Then you follow the track across the sand and sage of Antone Flat. When you start walking on sandstone again, cairns direct you right up the wash that has several natural tanks or water pockets. Climbing out of the wash, one more sand walk brings you to the descent down the slickrock. There is some ledge walking and then the route crosses over to the next hill. A boulder-strewn path drops you down the "E" hill to Pine Creek. The land along the creek is private land so stay on the east bank of Pine Creek and follow it south until it joins the Escalante River, then go upriver until it opens up. The exit route is against the southern wall. This leads to the trail register and the short spur road back to Highway 12.

# 10

# Burr Trail

## Map, Road Log, and Hikes

This road is paved to the edge of Capitol Reef National Park. It is not recommended for trailers due to the tight switchbacks through the Waterpocket Fold, a hundred-mile-long monocline. The road provides access to the highly colorful country of the Circle Cliffs. Most of this country was made accessible by the uranium boom of the 1950s.

| MILES | DESCRIPTION |
|---|---|
| 0.0 | Start of the Burr Trail |
| 6.4 | **HIKE 41: DEER CREEK.** The BLM has a campground on the north side of the road. |
| 10.1 | Trailhead parking (R) in 0.2 of a mile **HIKE 42: THE GULCH** |
| 10.7 | **HIKE 43: UPPER GULCH**, short loop road (L) |
| 12.1 | The road follows Long Canyon. The scenery changes from red to white as the Wingate cliffs dominate. |
| 17.6 | Pullout (R). View of the Circle Cliffs and the Henry Mountains. |
| 20.4 | Turn (R) to Horse, Wolverine, Little Death Hollow, Silver Falls Creek, and the Moody Canyons. |

    5.7    Road (R) to Horse Canyon
            **HIKE 44: HORSE CANYON**

    10.3    **HIKE 45: WOLVERINE CREEK.** No collecting of petrified wood. Black petrified logs are exposed on the purple ground.

    13.0    **HIKE 46: LITTLE DEATH HOLLOW**

    20.3    Signed junction. Road left goes north to the Burr Trail in 8.4 miles. Road right continues on to the Moody Canyons.

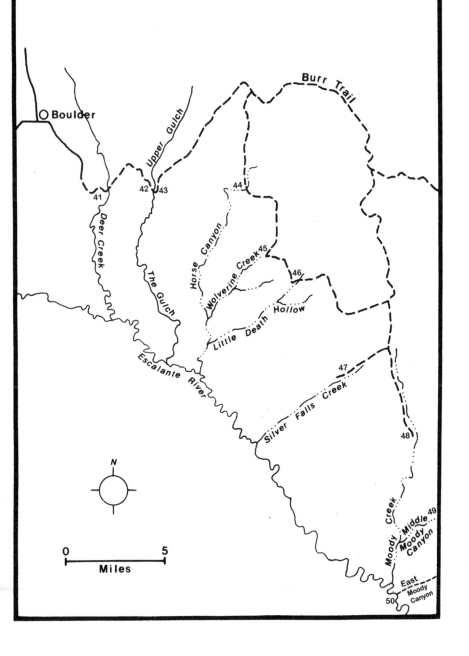

# THE BURR TRAIL

Boulder

Burr Trail

Upper Gulch

41

42 43

44

Deer Creek

The Gulch

Horse Canyon

Wolverine Creek 45

46

Little Death Hollow

Escalante River

47

Silver Falls Creek

48

Moody Creek

Middle 49
Moody
Canyon

East
Moody
Canyon

50

N

0        5
Miles

| | |
|---|---|
| 23.1 | Turnoff (R) to Silver Falls Creek |
| | **2.4   HIKE 47: SILVER FALLS CREEK** |
| 29.3 | Road is in the wash. |
| 32.8 | **HIKE 48: MOODY CANYON** Trailhead (R) |
| 36.0 | Unnamed road (R) |
| | **2.1   HIKE 49: MIDDLE MOODY CANYON** |
| | **HIKE 50: EAST MOODY CANYON** |
| 31.2 | Turnoff (R) to Silver Falls and Moody Canyons. Road goes 8.4 miles to the junction with the loop road from the Burr Trail. |
| 32.5 | End of pavement at Capitol Reef National Park |

## HIKE 41: DEER CREEK

Difficulty: Strenuous
Length (one way): 7.5 miles
Time: 1 day
Map: King Bench
Water: Deer Creek

This challenging route requires some deep wading and negotiating brush thickets. The reward is an intimate association with a lively stream and a colorful canyon. A serious, six-day loop trip can be made by continuing down the Escalante River (HIKE 7) and exiting up the Gulch (HIKE 42).

Drive 6.4 miles down the Burr Trail. The BLM has a campground on the north side of the road. Park on the right and head south along the stream bank.

The area is quite green; the banks of the stream are covered with scouring rushes. These primitive aquatic plants can be separated from their close relatives, the sedges, by the following jingle: "Sedges have edges and rushes are round." Both of these plants have three-ranked leaves. Because the scouring rushes contain high amounts of silica, the early settlers used them to clean their pots. Among the cattails (*Typha latifolia*) you may occasionally glimpse a red-winged blackbird (*Agelaius*

Water pocket filled with sticks

*phoeniceus*). These melodic birds are easily identified by their bright red-and-yellow shoulder patch.

Either side of the stream can be the jump-off point, but the west side offers a way along the sandy benches. This path can be followed for the first two miles, but when Deer Creek appears to run into Durffey Mesa, it is time to pick a route down to stream level. This can easily be done at the north side of the mouth of the second drainage coming in from the west.

The next mile or so of travel along the enclosed banks of the creek is heavily brushed, and it is often simpler to walk in the center of the stream. Walking in the creek bed stirs up a lot of silt. This stream seems to have a great deal of sediment, but it will probably get scoured during the summer monsoons. This makes for a challenging passage as the bottom is not visible.

The creek makes several more attempts to cut into the mesa, but its convoluted path leads it in a southerly direction. There is only one pool that is over waist deep, but the cool, dark water and the enclosed walls did not reassure me that a swim was not in the forecast.

After several more sharp bends, there is a track on the west bank for a quarter mile. This easier route gives you an opportunity to take a better look at the striated walls. Another mile of walking brings you to a small arch formed in a slab of rock that appears to have fractured away from the west wall. On the opposite shelf, a toadstool rock has been carved out of the unevenly weathered sandstone.

The nature of the stream changes as it flows over fluted red ledges. The water feels warmer and is certainly shallower. Those little elongated black specks that are attached to the submerged rocks are the larval stage of aquatic insects.

The last side drainage coming in from the east before Boulder Creek is worth a brief side trip. Although there are adequate campsites at several spots along Deer Creek, the first really good spot is located against the west wall just past the junction with Boulder Creek. Return the way you came or continue down Boulder Creek to the Escalante River to do the loop hike.

The Gulch

## HIKE 42: THE GULCH

Difficulty: Moderate
Length (one way): 12.5 miles
Time: 2 days
Maps: King Bench, Red Breaks
Water: The Gulch

This was the first canyon I hiked in the Escalante country. A flash flood has made the travel a bit more difficult, but it remains a beautiful place.

In just over 10 miles down the Burr Trail, there is a right turn that leads to trailhead parking in 0.2 mile. Follow the path down the hill to reach the Gulch. Head down the west side of the flowing stream. There's a fence in about an eighth of a mile. The red layers of the Kayenta quickly dip underground, and the domes and striated patterns of the lighter Navajo sandstone dominate the view.

After two miles of travel, there are a couple of caves carved out of the north wall. Two more miles and the canyon bends sharply to the

Halfway Hollow, the Gulch

east. The west bank has a short side drainage. The map says there is a spring but I only found wet sand.

A half mile after the Gulch swings south again, a pedestal rock looms on the horizon. This marker signals a sharp bend in the passage.

The canyon narrows in another mile, and for the next half mile you're caught between the sculptured walls as the stream cuts a way through. Right when there is a sharp turn to the east, the stream disappears down a constricted waterfall.

The first time I came to this notch where the water seems to disappear, I tried to negotiate the sloping sandstone ledge so I could avoid

Narrows, Lower Gulch

the murky pool at the end of this constriction. When I fell twelve feet with my backpack into this narrow gorge, I broke my foot on a boulder at the bottom. I ended up having to swim the pool anyway. Three days later I managed to hobble the rest of the way down the Gulch and up the Escalante River to the highway.

The next time around, a route around the narrows was found. It is worthwhile to walk this far and evaluate the water flow, your ability, and the time of year, take some pictures, and then decide whether to proceed or go back a ways and around. The route around starts about a sixteenth of a mile back up the canyon where there is a shallow alcove on the west wall.

There is a break in the wall. I've placed a cairn topped with two black rocks on the first ledge about twenty feet above the streambed. There was a log jammed against the side of the wall but it's an easy friction climb to start up the sandstone. Continue up the layered sandstone until you're on Brigham Tea Bench. Catch your breath and enjoy the stupendous views in all directions. Head south until you can look due east into the narrows that you are skirting. Off to the right and below the rim are several green benches. The third one is your destination. At eye level, a distinct knoll will protrude to the southeast. Contour along the rim, walking on sand but staying away from the immediate edge. There's a crack system that blocks further progress along the rim. This is the route down. Most of the way is simple. About two-thirds of the way down, which has been cairned, there's a small chimney where it is probably simpler to lower your pack down on a rope. When you get to the level bench, locate the cairn at the east end that indicates the short step down to creek level. By all means, take the time to go back up through the narrows.

Halfway Hollow almost immediately enters from the north. This challenging passage does not go far until you hit a jump. Rumor has it that a route around the narrows to the east will lead into similar constricted pour-offs farther up Halfway Hollow.

When the canyon goes through a narrow portal, the jammed cottonwood log about fifteen feet up gives you a further reason to pause and reflect on the tremendous force of moving water. There are some possible camp spots along this stretch and for the next half mile past the northern side drainage. Then the canyon narrows again.

Another three miles bring you to a challenging side trip. Along this narrow side fissure you can find some vegetation not seen along the main stream.

The tall grass with the silky tufts near the head is alkali sacaton (*Sporobolus airoides*). This grass has an open panicle, separating the seed grains along widely spreading branches.

Sacred datura (*Datura metaloides*) has long, white, funnel-shaped flowers that open in the evening. The prickly berries are the fruits. All parts of this plant contain alkaloid poisons but the psychedelic qualities were used by Indians in their religious ceremonies.

Before you have gone a half mile up this crack, climb out the south side and across the short, sandstone ridge to the next fissure. Follow this one back down to the Gulch.

There are plenty of campsites in the next mile of easy walking down to the Escalante River. The junction of the two streams is crowded with willows.

## HIKE 43: UPPER GULCH

Difficulty: Moderate
Length (one way): 10 miles
Time: 1 day
Maps: King Bench, Steep Creek Bench
Water: Water Canyon

This is one of the few hikes not aimed at getting to the Escalante River. The Wingate cliffs give way to open sagebrush benches as this canyon cuts through the multicolored Chinle Formation. A sharp contrast is provided by the narrow, deep, western side drainages. The last side canyon before Impossible Peak contains a massive arch.

Crossing the stream of the Gulch on the Burr Trail, take the short loop road to the left in 10.7 miles. Head up the streambed. In less than a mile, Steep Creek comes in on the left. Just before the mouth of this creek, there's a deep overhang on the west bank. Side passages provide many of the scenic marvels on this hike. Steep Creek is a very long drainage and deserves a day or two of exploration. The next narrow opening entering from the west branches about a half mile up. There was a large tree trunk jammed below the left slot.

The black streaks and orange patterns on the walls continue for another mile up the main canyon. You're forced to go around on the left when the water cuts through the Shinarump layer. The stair-step ends at a three-foot waterfall. The sandy, steep arroyo is the exit route to get above this constriction. A fence across the wash is the first thing that greets you when you've climbed up. A much more open canyon awaits you. The Gulch goes through several bow-knot meanders. Around the first bend there's a shallow cave cut out of the west wall, but cattle seem to have been the main visitors. The edge of the stream is a muddy bank.

When hiking this canyon, we saw the large, three-inch tracks of a mountain lion (*Felis concolor*). This elusive, nocturnal creature has been the basis of many myths. It is an effective predator, playing its part in the "balance of nature" by culling weak and diseased deer. Although constantly hunted, this much-maligned animal continues to share the

Lamanite Arch, Upper Gulch

wild, open spaces. The Incas called this creature *puma*. Early settlers on the East Coast called it *panther*.

There is a whole world of wonder right at your feet. The large, four-toed and ridge-shaped heel pad of the mountain lion and the pinpoints and tail scrapes of the northern whiptail lizard (*Cnemidophorus tigris septentrionalis*) in the mud and sand expose a whole different world. Because most of the mammals here are nocturnal, they are rarely seen. Even many of the other glimpses of wildlife are very fleeting. Deciphering these tracks can become an interesting game in unraveling the natural history of the creatures that inhabit these canyons. To a photographer, they also provide challenging form and texture photos.

Another short, western branch appears in a quarter mile. The main canyon continues to widen and serious benchland walking becomes the norm. These benches are covered with big sagebrush. This plant, the state flower of Nevada, thrives in deep, mildly basic soils. The small leaves, covered with grayish hairs, are adaptations for the retention of water under semiarid conditions. Belonging to the sunflower family, it does not follow the trends of most of the members by being insect pollinated but is instead wind pollinated. The genus name honors Artemisia, the

Convolutions in Upper Gulch

wife of Mausolus, an ancient ruler in Asia Minor who had a magnificent monument erected in his memory. Artemisia is derived from Artemis, the Greek goddess of wild nature. The fragrance of this damp plant is a recognizable western staple.

The next side branch, Water Canyon, provides the water flow for the Gulch. The streambed is filled with rushes and willows, which have been pushed down from a recent flash flood. About halfway up this dead-end canyon, a huge cave hangs inaccessibly on the cliff face. The terminal alcove is covered with columbine, watercress, and cattails.

Egg Canyon appears in two and a half miles. The Wingate cliffs frame the upper reaches of the canyon, but the purple mounds and pedestal rocks dominate the foreground. Explore this dry, eastern side drainage to uncover the reason for its name. A mile and a half up this wash, an old mining road becomes evident. At the crest of the hill, views of the Circle Cliffs and the Henry Mountains unfold.

Indian Trail Canyon appears on the left in another mile. A serious bushwhack up this constricted streambed is necessary to get a view of

Lamanite Arch, but it is well worth the effort to make this trip. This inaccessible arch is certainly the highlight of the hike. There may be water flowing in this canyon. The high bench near the mouth is a good campsite.

Arroyo cutting is evident as you work your way up the meanders of the Gulch. Roads left from uranium exploration are numerous as you approach the boundary to Forest Service lands. The pack trail marked on the map is difficult to locate in its lower reaches. An exposed, eighteen-foot pitch to get to the top of the Kayenta has a fixed rope dangling from the top. This is not the place to have an accident so I didn't try it. Climbing up to this spot, there's a triangular window in a separated slab of rock along the west wall of the immediate side gulch.

The jeep track continues up the Gulch, with views of Stair Canyon in the distance and the white dome of Impossible Peak to the west.

## HIKE 44: HORSE CANYON

Difficulty: Easy
Length (one way): 13 miles
Time: 1 to 2 days
Maps: Pioneer Mesa, King Bench, Red Breaks
Water: Lower Horse Canyon, Escalante River

This is the first of the canyons that drains the Circle Cliff Upwarp. The Circle Cliffs were uplifted during the Laramide Orogeny, which lasted from 50 to 80 million years ago. The present Rocky Mountains were formed during this time, and, closer to our area, the San Rafael Swell was uplifted. Wide near the head where it cuts through the easily erodible Chinle Formation, by the time Horse Canyon joins the Escalante it is enclosed by impressive walls. This long hike offers several exit routes pioneered by the cattlemen that bring you to the higher benchlands.

Head east from Boulder on the Burr Trail for 20.4 miles. At the sign, turn right. In 5.7 miles a road turns right for Horse Canyon. Since there has been work done on this road, it is possible to drive most of this hike and end up by the spring.

Holes in the wall, Horse Canyon

Being a hiker, I've left the route description the same starting from the turn-off. It looks like Horse Canyon is going to go straight through the Circle Cliffs to the west but the draw veers sharply to the south. It remains a wide wash until you pass the old mining claim marker, a white rectangle painted on the rock. The uranium boom in the 1950s brought extensive exploration throughout the area. The Bonneville Company did extensive drilling in Horse Canyon. Mine activity lasted from 1952 to 1956.

Chunks of petrified wood can be found in the streambed. At the first side draw coming in from the east, there is a nice oak grove at the mouth. This side slot is boulder strewn at the lower end, making it a challenge to explore. The air is filled with northern flickers (*Colaptes auratus*).

As the canyon starts to meander, the displays of desert varnish highlight the walls. Two miles of these twists and there are a couple of windows sculpted out of the sandstone cliff. A stock fence is strung across the wash around the next bend.

This signals the start of a narrow section. The next side slot plunges dramatically into Horse Canyon through a cleft in the cliff about thirty feet above the canyon floor. Going around the next rock outcropping, you pass by a display of little arches, alcoves, and other scooped-out pockets along the west wall.

This brief and intense passage ends quickly and the wash opens up again. Wolverine Creek (HIKE 45) comes in from the east in three more bends.

The wide sandy spaces last for another half mile and then sagebrush covers the sand benches. Around a sharp bend, there's an overhang on the northwest wall that makes an excellent camp spot. The shallow overhang has several Fremont barberry bushes (*Mahonia fremontii*) that act as vegetative screening. The fragrance from the small, yellow flowers is an added treat. Also known as holly-grape, this is closely related to the state flower for Oregon. The small, dark blue berries can be made into excellent jams and jellies. A yellow dye is made from the roots and stems.

Across the way is a pack trail climbing up the hillside. When the trail forks, either direction takes you to a spring, and there is a line camp by the right route. The spring on the left is developed and generally has a better flow. Continue on the pack trail past the water trough until it breaks to the top of Little Bown Bench for a larger view. In the next bend of Horse, surface water appears.

At the fence just around the next bend, a BLM road closure sign ends travel down the canyon. Another half mile and the mouth of Little Death Hollow (HIKE 46) appears from the east. The generator and sections of old pipe were part of an attempt to get water for cattle up to Big Bown Bench. Another fence spans Horse Canyon a quarter mile farther down.

The next short fissure entering from the east is choked with vegetation. The upper portion is boulder strewn.

From here, another fifteen minutes of walking brings you to the wide junction with the Escalante River.

Petrified wood, Wolverine Canyon

## HIKE 45: WOLVERINE CREEK

Difficulty: Moderate
Length (one way): 5 miles
Time: 1 day
Maps: Pioneer Mesa, King Bench
Water: Bring your own

This area is noted for its black petrified wood and a portion was set aside by the BLM as an outstanding natural area. The lower portion has extensive honeycombed walls.

Travel 20.4 miles down the Burr Trail. Turn right at the sign and continue another 10.3 miles. The route starts at the BLM sign detailing the scenic qualities of the area and reminding visitors that this area is closed to collecting. The black petrified wood attracts the eye because the purple and lavender hills provide such a vibrant backdrop. Climb over the fence where the steps are provided.

The first mile and a half of easy walking take you through the Circle Cliffs and a junction with the most northerly arm. Petrified wood pieces are scattered throughout the hillsides. It is easiest to cut across the benches rather than follow the meanders of the wash.

Turning south, in another mile the south fork joins Wolverine Creek. The gray beds at the junction provide a good seat for a pause in which to gaze at the cliffs starting to surround you.

Intermittent water occurs shortly down-canyon, creating conditions for cottonwoods and other riparian plants to appear. Two large alcoves have been eroded out of the northern bends.

The walls of the lower canyon are highly eroded with small pockets, some of which are deep enough to sit in. These windows and honeycombed basins look as if scoops have been taken out of the sandstone walls. Vertical cracks take the eye to the sky and stain patterns higher up.

The last half mile doubles back on itself and the sand slows down the pace. The canyon opens just as it joins Horse Canyon.

## HIKE 46: LITTLE DEATH HOLLOW

Difficulty: Strenuous
Length (one way): 7.5 miles
Time: 1 day
Maps: Pioneer Mesa, Silver Falls Bench, Red Breaks
Water: Bring your own

Although this canyon is named Death Hollow, its name has been altered to differentiate it from the much longer and more strenuous canyon (HIKE 38) draining the Aquarius Plateau. This hike offers a superb section of narrows, an oval arch, an extremely tight lateral passage, and Indian petroglyphs.

Take the Burr Trail for 20.4 miles to the signed junction. Go right for 13 miles. Take the short spur west to the corral. The route starts here. After crossing the fence, stay on the grassy area to the right (north) of the wash. Juniper and sage dot the landscape. In a mile and a half of easy walking, the south fork joins the arroyo. Another mile and a narrower, convoluted channel dominates, with colorful sandstone walls enclosing the canyon.

Little Death Hollow                Footprints

There are lateral joints leading away from the main canyon. Look for the oval arch in one of the remnant fins left between two of these parallel fissures. It's one of those sights that holds you because it is superlative in an already highly scenic area.

After a few more twisting meanders, a narrow slot appears on the north wall. You can climb over the first blockage and continue around the bend. The next slot is sloped as it winds around the curve, calling for a sideways stemming technique.

The walls of the main canyon stay straight, but the wash bottom narrows to a six-foot width. We were surprised to see a kangaroo rat (*Dipodomys ordi*) hopping down the narrow channel. This rodent has evolved so that it is able to survive in a desert environment. It has no need for drinking water, since it is able to extract water from the seeds that it eats. Spacious, convoluted chambers behind the nose condense water vapor from the air.

For the next mile and a half, the canyon remains one serious constriction. Up to this point, the streambed itself has been fairly flat and gravelly. Now there are some boulder jams. Depending on the water, there are routes around them.

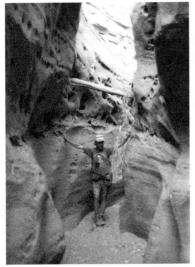

Little Death Hollow

Hiking companions

Arch in Little Death Hollow

The last boulder was bypassed on the ledge that then sloped down to the canyon floor.

The drainage widens and in another mile you pass under an old pipeline that carried water up to Big Bown Bench. The wide mouth of Little Death Hollow bears little resemblance to the just completed narrows. The junction with Horse Canyon is the first safe place to camp.

To complete the loop hike, head up Horse Canyon (HIKE 44) and out Wolverine Creek (HIKE 45).

## HIKE 47: SILVER FALLS CREEK

Difficulty: Moderate
Length (one way): 8.5 miles
Time: 1 day
Maps: Horse Pasture Mesa, Scorpion Gulch
Water: Escalante River

This beautiful canyon was part of the Hall's Crossing Road that was used to get to southeastern Utah after the Hole-in-the-Rock route was abandoned. The transformation from wide wash to narrow canyon is typical for the canyons draining the Circle Cliffs. The lower portion of the canyon is adorned with great streaks of desert varnish, giving this canyon its name.

Drive down the Burr Trail to the signed turnoff in 20.4 miles. Turn right and go another 20.3 miles. At the junction with the road going left to the Burr Trail, go right for another 2.8 miles. Turn right for Silver Falls Creek.

In about two and a half miles, the corral on the right is a good place to park. This whole canyon used to be a four-wheel-drive route that connected with Harris Wash as a cross-canyon trail. With the passage of legislation authorizing Glen Canyon National Recreation Area, this road is now closed.

Just past the corral, the old jeep track climbs up the hill to avoid a meander of the drainage that plunges through and over the gray Shinarump bedrock. This half-mile bend is an eroded wonderland of

G. B. Hobbs inscription, Silver Falls Canyon

windows and scooped-out pockets in the rocks. Explore this without a backpack as it takes a scramble to get down the first drop-off.

Following the track, the purple, red, gray, and green shades of the exposed oxides of the iron-bearing minerals create a lively background. This rock layer also contains uranium ore, so there was intense exploration and mining activity in the 1950s wherever this formation was exposed at the surface. The rock cairns are old mining claim boundary markers.

Shortly after the north fork comes in, the GCNRA sign is visible. The rising walls of Wingate come closer together. It seems like an anomaly that this is the same rock formation that is perched high above stream level just a few miles back. The area of the Circle Cliffs is an upwarp, which means that the land has been raised.

Just as the walls and the silence start to close in, a half-dozen cackling ravens (*Corvus corax*) pass by overhead. These opportunistic scavengers are very common. Continuing deeper into the canyon, you pass by a rincon on either side. These high and dry meanders are part of the readable history of the stream. The spring marked on the topographic map is just a slight seep but water does appear shortly down-canyon.

In another mile the Hobbs inscription and memorial plaque are found in an overhang on the west wall. George Brigham Hobbs was with the Hole-in-the-Rock expedition and was one of the four scouts sent to

Formation in Silver Falls Canyon

explore the unknown country east of the Colorado River. He was taking supplies to the settlers at Bluff in February of 1883 when he was caught in a snowstorm. Figuring that his time had come, he pecked his name in the sandstone. He survived and was able to complete his journey.

In the last two miles the canyon widens, and benches that are suitable campsites appear. The corral on the right means the river is a quarter of a mile away.

## HIKE 48: MOODY CANYON

Difficulty: Moderate
Length (one way): 7 miles
Time: 1 day
Maps: Horse Pasture Mesa, Scorpion Gulch
Water: Escalante River

This canyon provides access into the lower part of the Escalante River. The colorful hills give way to a boulder-strewn canyon.

From the Boulder turnoff, drive on the Burr Trail for 20.4 miles. Turn right for 20.3 miles to the junction. Continue for another 9.7 miles to where the road leaves the wash and turns east. The last 3.5 miles are in Moody Creek wash and may be sandy. The corral may be the best spot to park. Start down the wash.

The wash is quite wide as you start hiking southwest. The multicolored hills are topped with white monoliths. After two and a half miles of walking, a box canyon comes in from the west. Seasonal water pockets may be found about halfway up this short draw. Another mile and there is an arch just past the mouth of the next side arm. One more mile and the wide entrance to Middle Moody Canyon appears.

Continuing down the Moody Creek drainage, the Wingate sandstone encloses the canyon for the remaining two and a half miles. There are several stretches where big blocks have fallen from the walls, but a way

Middle Moody Canyon

through them is easily found. After the last boulder field, the channel straightens and you can hear the river. Camping is best near the mouth.

## HIKE 49: MIDDLE MOODY CANYON

Difficulty: Moderate
Length (one way): 4.5 miles
Time: 1 day
Maps: Horse Pasture Mesa, Deer Point, Scorpion Gulch
Water: Escalante River

This hike provides another opportunity to explore the colorful formations found in the Circle Cliffs. Combining this hike with East Moody Canyon (HIKE 50) for a two- to three-day loop will provide greater variety. It can also be explored going up-canyon toward Deer Point.

Take the Burr Trail for 20.4 miles. Turn right at the sign and go 20.3 miles to the junction leading back to the Burr Trail. Turn right for another 12.9 miles. Turn right and go 2.1 miles to the drill pad.

Deer skull

If you want to go down into the narrows, pick a route carefully down the side draw and boulders to the canyon floor. An alternate entry is to walk down-canyon on the closed mining track to where it intersects the wash.

The wash down-canyon opens up. You can follow cattle trails across the benchland to avoid the meanders in the wash. The Chinle Formation provides the color on the low clay hills. As the wash widens, the sandy benches are covered with cheatgrass (*Bromus tectorum*), tumbleweed (*Salsola kali*), and rabbitbrush.

Then the wash curves around a large, colorful dome. Pedestal formations line the canyon. In about two hours the junction with Moody Canyon comes in from the right. Continue to the river if you are doing the loop.

If you want to head up-canyon, it is a 5-mile hike one-way to the base of Deer Point. Head up the narrows. As the walls rise higher, the wash opens up a bit. Utah juniper and Apache plume (*Fallugia paradoxa*) cover the slopes. Exercise care in this area as the wash floor is rocky. It is always the one that looks the most stable that moves when you step on it.

At the fork, not the short side arm where the canyon heads north, the left branch is the main one. There is a brief burst of red and purple

East Moody Canyon

shales at stream level, but the wash debris quickly covers most of the color. Fallen boulders add to the challenge of finding a route. Then the streambed composition changes to brown ledges with fossilized ripple marks.

Tracks of bighorn sheep (*Ovis canadensis*) were found in the soft mud. These animals were transplanted from the upper portions of Lake Powell and seem to be doing well.

After two more miles, the walls diminish in height. I scrambled up the wall on the right to the flat area above. On top, a whole different landscape unfolds. There are many shallow draws that are filled with the yellows and reds of Gambel oak and skunkbush sumac in the fall.

Two more miles in the wash brings you to the base of Deer Point.

## HIKE 50: EAST MOODY CANYON

Difficulty: Moderate
Length (loop): 18 miles
Time: 2 to 3 days
Maps: Horse Pasture Mesa, Deer Point, Scorpion Gulch, Stevens
    Canyon North
Water: Escalante River

This canyon can be combined with the Middle Moody Canyon Hike for a two- to three-day round trip or it can be reached through a break in the Wingate cliffs following an old mining track from the Middle Moody trailhead.

From the mouth of Moody Canyon follow the Escalante River for two stream crossings. This will put you back on the east side of the river. A path worn by hikers will lead you up and around to the mouth of East Moody Canyon. There are good camp spots at the mouth. In the first bend there is a large, shallow alcove. The next bend has a really photogenic wall. Camping near the streambed, I found a fifteen-foot tunnel in a fallen boulder to stuff my gear. When the clouds turned to snow, I joined my gear.

You may find water in the first right arm but the streambed is dry from here as the canyon starts to open up. At the third north arm, turn left. There is a short boulder pile to negotiate. Purple beds and petrified wood appear. In two miles, evidence of the mining track appears at the junction with the north arm. This route climbs steeply along the Wingate boulders to a break in the cliff face at the head of this arm. The view is stupendous from this saddle. It took me two and a half hours to get down the Chinle slopes, past the mine remains, skirting the narrows of Middle Moody Canyon to where the track crosses the wash. This closes the loop. Either follow the track back to the trailhead or go to the narrows and climb out the first left slot.

# References

Abbey, Edward, and Philip Hyde. *Slickrock: The Canyon Country of Southeast Utah.* San Francisco: Sierra Club, 1971.

Ambler, J. Richard. *The Anasazi.* Flagstaff, AZ: Museum of Northern Arizona, 1971.

Baars, Donald L. *Red Rock Country.* Garden City, NY: Doubleday, 1972.

———. *A Traveler's Guide to the Geology of the Colorado Plateau.* Salt Lake City: University of Utah Press, 2002.

Barnes, F. A., and Michaelene Pendleton. *Canyon Country Prehistoric Indians.* Salt Lake City, UT: Wasatch Publishers, 1979.

Breed, Jack. "First Motor Sortie into Escalante Land." *National Geographic* 96 (1949): 369–404.

Chan, Marjorie A., and William T. Parry. *Rainbow Rocks: Mysteries of Sandstone Colors and Concretions in Colorado Plateau Canyon Country.* Public Information Series 77, Utah Geological Survey. Salt Lake City: University of Utah, 2002.

Chesher, Greer K. *Heart of the Desert Wild: Grand Staircase–Escalante National Monument.* Bryce Canyon, UT: Bryce Canyon Natural History Association, 2000.

Chidester, Ida, and E. Bruhn. "A History of Garfield County." *Garfield County News,* Panguitch, UT, 1949.

Clark, Deborah J. *Capitol Reef Wildflowers.* El Dorado Hills, CA: Impact Photographics, Inc., 2009.

Crampton, C. Gregory. "Military Reconnaissance in Southern Utah, 1866." *Utah Historical Quarterly* 32, no. 2 (1964): 145–61.

———. *Standing Up Country.* New York: Alfred A. Knopf, 1964.

Fagan, Damian. *Canyon Country Wildflowers.* Helena, MT: Falcon Publishing Co., 1998.

Fillmore, Robert. *The Geology of the Parks, Monuments, and Wildlands of Southern Utah.* Salt Lake City: University of Utah Press, 2000.

Fleischner, Thomas Lowe. *Singing Stone: A Natural History of the Escalante Canyons.* Salt Lake City: University of Utah Press, 1999.

Gregory, Herbert E. "Scientific Explorations in Southern Utah." *American Journal of Science* 243 (1945): 529–49.

Hayward, C. Lynn, D. Elden Beck, and Wilmer W. Tanner. *Zoology of the Upper Colorado River Basin: I. The Biotic Communities.* Brigham

Young University Science Bulletin, Biological Series, Vol. 1, No. 3. Provo, UT: Brigham Young University, 1958.

Henderson, Randall. "When the Boats Wouldn't Float—We Pulled 'em." *Desert Magazine* (September 1950): 5–13.

Howard, Lynn. *Utah's Wilderness Areas: The Complete Guide.* Englewood, CO: Wildlife Publishers, Inc., 2005.

Le Fevre, Lenora. *Boulder Country and Its People.* Springville, UT: Art City Publishers, 1973.

Mantle, Jens. *Arches of the Escalante Canyons and Kaiparowits Plateau, Grand Staircase—Escalante National Monument.* Thompson Springs, UT: Arch Hunter Books, 2002.

Martrès, Laurent. *Photographing the Southwest.* 2d ed. Volume 1: *A Guide to the Natural Landmarks of Southern Utah.* Alta Loma, CA: Photo Trip USA, 2002.

Miller, David E. *Hole-in-the-Rock.* Salt Lake City: University of Utah Press, 1966.

Moore, Robert, W. "Escalante: Utah's River of Arches." *National Geographic* 108 (1955): 399–418.

Porter, Elliot. *The Place No One Knew: Glen Canyon on the Colorado.* San Francisco: Sierra Club, 1963.

Rabkin, Richard, and Jacob Rabkin. *Nature in the West.* New York: Holt, Rinehart and Winston, 1981.

Rusho, W. L. *Everett Ruess: A Vagabond for Beauty.* Salt Lake City, UT: Peregrine Smith Books, 1983.

Slifer, Dennis. *Guide to Rock Art of the Utah Region: Sites with Public Access.* Santa Fe, NM: Ancient City Press, 2000.

Smith, Gibbs. *On Desert Trails with Everett Ruess.* Commemorative edition. Layton, UT: Gibbs Smith Publisher, 2000.

Walka, Ann Weiler. *Walking the Unknown: River and Other Travels in Escalante Country.* Flagstaff, AZ: Bluff City Books, 2002.

Williams, Brooke. *Escalante: The Best Kind of Nothing.* Tucson: University of Arizona Press, 2006.

Woodbury, Angus M. *Ecological Studies of Flora and Fauna in Glen Canyon.* University of Utah Anthropological Papers No. 40, Glen Canyon Series No. 7. Salt Lake City: University of Utah Press, 1959.

Woolsey, Nethella G. *The Escalante Story (1875–1964).* Springville, UT: Art City Publishers, 1964.

# Biographical Sketch

Born in the Netherlands, Rudi Lambrechtse immigrated to the United States as a young child. Family summer vacations brought an early appreciation for the tremendous diversity this country had to offer. This wanderlust remains as a central aspect of the author's character.

Lambrechtse came out west in the 1970s and has lived in Arizona for the last thirty-five years. After completing a Master's degree in biology at Northern Arizona University, he worked in the Grand Canyon for eight seasons as a trail and river guide. Recently retired after twenty years as an elementary school teacher, he is still hiking and running rivers.